We're called to be fishers of men— even our best efforts produce no results. In *Purple Fish*, Mark Wilson suggests we need to relearn the way we're fishing. He teaches an approach to evangelism that will draw you closer to Jesus as you talk about him with others. If you're being called to the deeper water, where the fish are plenty but the struggle is great, this is the guide you need.

—MARK BATTERSON, *New York Times* bestselling author and lead pastor, National Community Church

Mark Wilson takes you on a memorable fishing trip and treasure hunt that will motivate you to reengage in God's mission with a new sense of vigor. This book is witty, engaging, down to earth, and transformative!

—JR WOODWARD, national director, The V3 Church Planting Movement, author of *Creating a Missional Culture*

We must relearn personal evangelism. The "old way" doesn't work—everyone knows that. In *Purple Fish*, Mark Wilson offers an approach he lives and teaches and that can also work for you. Whether learning for yourself or training others in personal evangelism, this book is invaluable to that end. Bold as Love.

—BOB ROBERTS, SR., pastor NorthWood Church, author of *Bold as Love: What Can Happen When We See People the Way God Does*

You will never read a more fun or helpful book on evangelism than *Purple Fish*. The most reprinted book in English after the King James Bible is a fishing manual entitled *The Compleat Angler* (1653). This little classic on another kind of "fishing" deserves a similar future.

—LEONARD SWEET, best-selling author, professor (Drew University, George Fox University), and chief contributor to sermons.com

Purple Fish gets us to the heart of Jesus. Too long we have had formulas in sharing our faith. Mark takes us back to the Jesus model with compelling contemporary stories of doubt, faith, fear, and the presence of Christ. I personally was "spurred on" to joyously live and share the Jesus life.

—JO ANNE LYON, General Superintendent, The Wesleyan Church

Purple Fish is an adventure-filled read that helps alleviate the fears and misgivings about what it means for a follower of Jesus to tell someone else about Jesus. *Purple Fish* is a refreshing reminder, with practical witnessing tools, that Jesus saves and our privilege is to come alongside others to do what Jesus commands: to make disciples of all nations!

—JIM DUNN, Executive Director, Church Multiplication
and Discipleship, The Wesleyan Church

You don't have to like fishing to read *Purple Fish*, and you don't need to be an evangelist at heart. If you believe that God could use you to reach people, even just one, this book is for you.

—DAN REILAND, executive pastor,
12Stone Church, author of *Amplified Leadership*

Purple Fish inspires me to share my faith without shaming the sinner or stressing me out. Mark is what's needed today—a folk-theologian, a personalized pastor, an everyman's evangelist. Meaning: you can actually understand what he's saying in *Purple Fish*, and it matters. It might matter more than anything else.

—DAVID DRURY, author of several books including
Being Dad and Chief of Staff of The Wesleyan Church

Purple Fish is like an engaging conversation with a trusted friend and mentor in a Northwoods coffee shop. Mark Wilson warmly shares his heart and wisdom . . . and the good news continues to spread.

—WAYNE SCHMIDT, vice-president,
Wesley Seminary at Indiana Wesleyan University

Mark Wilson draws together insights from decades of helping ordinary people discover a love for about Jesus. *Purple Fish* shows how sharing one's faith is a journey into a deeper relationship with Christ as well as people in need.

—BOB WHITESEL, professor of missional leadership,
Wesley Seminary at Indiana Wesleyan University, author of
The Healthy Church and *Cure for the Common Church*

Mark does a masterful job of weaving stories and strategies into a seamless tapestry of sharing Jesus. *Purple Fish* is a must-read for anyone who desires to have their heart warmed for sharing the good news of Jesus Christ.

—PHIL STEVENSON, assistant district superintendent
Pacific-Southwest District, The Wesleyan Church

Fishing and evangelism are two things I've never been a big fan of. And after reading *Purple Fish*, I think I'll take up both. This book will warm your heart and give you a whole new perspective of Jesus' Great Commission. I love it. Now all I need, is a rod and reel.

—KEITH LOY, lead pastor, Celebrate Community Church

Wonderfully engaging vignettes, apt literary quotations, and richly practical insights on sharing Jesus with others make *Purple Fish* a true delight to read. This gem of a book is marked by the touch of the Holy Spirit and is an important read for those who want to learn better how to winsomely tell others of Jesus.

—EVVY HAY CAMPBELL, PhD, Board Chair, World Hope International

Purple Fish will challenge and inspire you to become more effective in fishing for people. Jesus came to seek and save the lost. This must become our passion as Christ's followers.

—THOMAS H. HERMIZ, General Superintendent for
the Churches of Christ in Christian Union

Purple Fish presents a non-judgmental, engaging and delightful approach to sharing Christ with others by Mark Wilson, a Northwoods pastor who practices what he preaches. You will love this book!

—BRAD JOHNSON, pastor of California Community Church

I loved this book! Mark Wilson makes the fishing metaphor soar with many of the best thinking and practices employed by those who share the gospel. If you are called be fishers of souls, this book will be a delight to read and study.

—HENRY REYENGA, JR., president of Christian Leaders Institute

Jesus said, "Follow me and I will make you fishers of men." *Purple Fish* is a great fishing guide for spiritual anglers.

— AL LINDNER, Hall of Fame angler and host of Angling Edge TV

As a fisherman, I love this book! The life of a fisherman can be filled with great struggle. Sharing Jesus with others is often no different, with multiple factors outside of our control affecting our efforts. In *Purple Fish*, Mark O. Wilson shares a simple strategy for evangelism that is unique and authentic, delivered with warmth and engagement, like you are having a conversation with an old friend.

— BENJI KELLEY, founding senior pastor, newhope church

To those who want to be Christ's ambassadors in this needy world (and that should be all of us who claim to be followers of Jesus): make way for Mark Wilson and his purple fish lessons. You'll learn how natural it can be to talk about God and build relationships with those who believe differently through embracing our common humanity, encouragement and love. And that is always good news!

— MARY SCHALLER, president, Q Place

PURPLE FISH

A HEART FOR SHARING JESUS

Mark O. Wilson

wesleyan
PUBLISHING HOUSE
wphstore.com

Copyright © 2014 by Mark O. Wilson
Published by Wesleyan Publishing House
Indianapolis, Indiana 46250
Printed in the United States of America
ISBN: 978-0-89827-910-8
ISBN (e-book): 978-0-89827-911-5

Library of Congress Cataloging-in-Publication Data

Wilson, Mark O.
Purple fish : a heart for sharing Jesus / Mark O. Wilson.
    pages cm
Includes bibliographical references.
ISBN 978-0-89827-910-8 (pbk.)
1. Witness bearing (Christianity) 2. Evangelistic work. 3. Missions. I. Title.
BV4520.W53 2014
248'.5--dc23

                        2014002997

To my fishing buddies

CONTENTS

For free shepherding resources,
visit www.wphresources.com/purplefish.

ACKNOWLEDGEMENTS

Thank you to . . .

Jesus, our ultimate purple fish, and Izaak Walton, the patron saint of fishing.

My lovely wife, Cathy, who flows with goodness, grace, and wisdom.

My delightful children, Adam, Ryan and Stacy, Luke and Emily, Wes and Jeweleeann, and Hannah for making many great memories. I am so proud of you.

Gail Godwin, whose writing inspired the purple fish idea.

My dear friend, Wayne Richards, who first gave me the opportunity to teach evangelism and is now working with me to publish good tidings.

My fantastic editor, Kevin Scott, who went the extra mile, and Famous Dave Anderson for arranging a Grand Pines cabin for our writing retreat.

Wayne MacBeth, Craig Bubeck, Jeff Ray, Dane Benton, Lyn Rayn, Rachael Stevenson, Susan LeBaron, and the rest of the Wesleyan Publishing House gang for your helpful assistance with this project.

Those who graciously granted permission to share their stories.

The Happy Old Men's Club, Nate and Steve, for the friendship, wisdom, and laughter.

Cody Conner, Larry Ramsell, Wendy Williamson, Dennis Waystedt, Robert Schuster, Jim January, and Mark Jalovick for your helpful fishing insights.

Nick Lyons for the fabulous angling quotes sprinkled throughout the book.

Jo Anne Lyon, Jim Dunn, Russ Gunsalus, and Dennis Jackson for believing in me and granting your blessing.

My FLAME Evangelism students, who had the courage to go on treasure hunts.

Steve Britton for giving me the coolest purple fish stick ever.

Hayward Wesleyan Church, coworkers and friends, for sharing many blessings over two decades.

PART 1

BIG FISH
AND
LOST TREASURES

MANY MEN GO FISHING ALL OF THEIR LIVES WITHOUT
KNOWING THAT IT IS NOT FISH THEY ARE AFTER.

—HENRY DAVID THOREAU

GO DOWN TO THE LAKE AND THROW IN A LINE.
OPEN THE MOUTH OF THE FIRST FISH YOU CATCH,
AND YOU WILL FIND A LARGE SILVER COIN.

—MATTHEW 17:27 NLT

1
SNAGGED
ON THE
LOST RIVER

THERE'S A FINE LINE BETWEEN FISHING AND JUST
STANDING ON THE SHORE LIKE AN IDIOT.

—STEVEN WRIGHT

Woodrow Wilson took me fishing when I was seven years old.
Daddy's brother, Uncle Woody, was named after the US president
who took office in 1913. Whenever we vacationed in southern
Indiana, I imagined it to be a White House visit. It felt presidential,
though I never could find the Lincoln Bedroom.

One day, Uncle Woody, who reminded me somewhat of the
rooster Foghorn Leghorn, asked me if I liked to fish. He was

flabbergasted upon hearing that I had never cast a line: "I declare, boy, that's a tragedy! Every kid needs to go fishing, and we're going to take care of that today." So Uncle Woody dug up some worms in a soup can, rigged a couple of poles, and took my brother Timmy and me to the Lost River in his Ford pickup.

Standing in soggy riverbank weeds, Uncle Woody handed us poles with squiggly worms on the hook and said, "Push the little button and cast over there."

Timmy did great, but I flubbed it. After four or five miserable attempts, Uncle Woody snatched the pole from my hand.

"No! No! That's not how it's done. Watch closely, boy, and I'll show you exactly what to do."

He drew back and let the line fly—straight up—into the limbs of the towering oak above us, and let out some Wesleyan Methodist expletives.

"Dagummit! Fiddlesticks!"

The fishing line tangled around a branch and dangled far above our heads. Befuddled, Uncle Woody sputtered and jerked the pole to no avail.

Eventually, he boosted Timmy into the tree for a search and rescue mission, but the line was far beyond his reach. I just watched forlornly in the hot August sun.

After a half hour of futile efforts, Uncle Woody finally had enough. He yanked hard, snapped the line, and left the bobber and worm swinging happily in the tree. Stuffing us back into his pickup, a sullen Uncle Woody drove home in silence.

Now, Uncle Woody was a kindhearted soul who truly wanted me to discover the joys of fishing. I'm sure he caught plenty of pan fish on other excursions. But our fishing expedition on the Lost River inspired no love within me for the sport.

On the dusty drive back to the White House, I decided fishing was not for me. "After all," I thought, "it's no fun, a frustrating waste of time, and the pressure is almost unbearable."

And that's how most Christians view evangelism.

We believe we should share our deeply held faith, but don't know how. We bumble around awkwardly when speaking about spiritual matters. When we fail in our attempts to fish the "Lost River," the natural conclusion is that witnessing is for a few other, super-spiritual saints, and not for ordinary folks like us.

Most Christ-followers are gracious people and don't want to be offensive or pushy. So they remain passive, feel guilty about their evangelism avoidance, and break into hives whenever the subject comes up.

As Becky Pippert noted, "Christians and non-Christians have something in common: we're both uptight about evangelism."[1]

In fact, I hesitate to even say this book is about evangelism for a couple reasons: (1) Thoughtful people are suspicious of those things that end with -*ism*. Sticking an "ism" on the end of something kills it and makes it a "was'm"; and (2) *evangelism* invites caricatures.

When I ask ministerial students whether the word *evangelism* carries positive or negative connotations, the response is usually 85 percent negative. *Evangelism* and *evangelist* bring mental pictures of televised money grubbers, abrasive fundamentalists, manipulative proselytizing, or simplistic religious formulas. No wonder it seems so unappealing.

Isn't there a better way?

ANOTHER KIND OF FISHING

Moving to northern Wisconsin forced me to get over my fishing aversion. Locals are convinced Hayward is the fishing capital of the universe. They take it quite seriously. And when in Hayward, you do as the Haywardites do.

During my first summer in the Northwoods, new friends took me to the water and taught me to cast. I quickly discovered there's more to fishing than the Uncle Woody method. I actually had fun, caught fish, and looked forward to the next trip.

ANOTHER KIND OF EVANGELISM

What if I told you there is a different way to share the gospel? What if we discovered an authentic, relational, no-pressure approach that is engaging, adventurous, and really works? Would you be interested? *Purple Fish* provides that.

Over the years, I've helped hundreds of people find Jesus, and trained many others with the perspectives presented in this spiritual fishing guidebook. I'm happy to share them with you.

Care to join me? If so, grab your pole, come along, and I'll let you in on the purple fish secret.

2
THE
PURPLE FISH
SECRET

THE MUSIC OF ANGLING IS MORE COMPELLING TO ME
THAN ANYTHING CONTRIVED IN THE GREATEST SYM-
PHONY HALL.

—A. J. MCCLANE

Do you wonder why this book is called *Purple Fish*? Though fishermen do not commonly divulge their secrets, I'll let you in on mine. It's a secret worth sharing. *Purple Fish* is mostly about attitude and perspective, rather than technique.

There are two great metaphors for sharing the gospel: fishing and treasure hunting. The purple fish combines both.

FISHING

Fishing fits naturally. Jesus loved fishing. He called Galilean anglers to follow him and fish for people. The *ichthus* symbol (fish) was used by the earliest Christians long before landing on evangelical bumper stickers.

The fishing image works for me personally as well. Hayward, my Northwoods home, is famous for world record muskies, and the Freshwater Fishing Hall of Fame. One of my favorite hobbies is dropping a line for bluegills on Nelson Lake or wader fishing in the Namekagon River. I also keep a fish count on my blog, recording a tally of each species caught by members of the Wilson tribe each summer. For us, fishing is a spiritual activity, like Norman Maclean expressed in *A River Runs through It*: "In our family, there was no clear line between religion and fly fishing."[1]

TREASURE HUNTING

Treasure, the other image, is equally compelling. Jesus said the kingdom of God is like a great treasure buried in a field (Matt. 13:44). It is of priceless value and worth the all-out search. In my evangelism courses, this theme plays a significant role, as we actually go out "treasure hunting" with amazing results. (You will read about that in chapter 32.)

So, I was in a quandary. Which metaphor should I use in this book on sharing Jesus with others: fishing or treasure hunting?

KALCHAINO: THE PURPLE FISH

The answer came from Gail Godwin's novel *Evensong*. I found it in the words of seminary professor, Dr. Stroup: "There's an interesting Greek word, *kalchaino*. . . . Literally, it means 'to search for the purple fish.' . . . The literal purple fish was a shellfish highly prized by the Greeks for its rich purple dye. . . . Divers went to the bottom of the sea in search of this elusive fish. That's how 'searching for the purple fish' came to be the Greeks' expression for plumbing the depths of one's mind."[2]

"*Kalchaino!*" I actually shouted, "Fishing and treasure hunting come together in one purple fish!"

I embarked on a study of purple fish and made several fascinating discoveries. The Tyrians (and later the Greeks) ventured forth onto high seas in search of the precious murex shellfish. When they found it, they would extract a rare purple dye, which was used for royal and priestly garments. Tyrian purple was "high-end" stuff. In other words, they were fishing for treasure.

This purple dye appears over fifty times throughout Scripture, notably in the tabernacle and temple curtains, priestly garments, and the robe placed on Jesus at the crucifixion. In Acts, we discover Lydia, an evangelist merchant of purple cloth (Acts 16:14–15).

So, for my purposes this is the definition of purple fish: something of great value worth seeking that when discovered brings great delight.

Unfortunately, for most Christians, evangelism feels more like a trip to the dentist than a purple fish fishing adventure. For years, that's the way I understood it because of negative personal experiences.

3
EVANGELISM MISADVENTURES

A MAN CAN ACTUALLY BECOME SO CAUGHT UP IN FISH-
ING
THAT IT ACTUALLY BECOMES A GRIM BUSINESS.

—SPARSE GREY HACKLE

I spent years being uptight about evangelism. My evangelical subculture declared the duty of good Christians was to win the lost at any cost. I wanted to please Jesus but somehow flunked the training courses. And like so many Christians, I abhorred witnessing and felt guilty about it.

MY FIRST SOUL-WINNING ATTEMPT

My first adolescent attempt at evangelism was a dismal failure. I signed up for a bicycle mission trip in Ohio with a dozen other enthusiastic fundamentalists from youth camp. We received a crash course in the Jack Hyles soul-winning method and were sent for a week on ten-speeds to convert as many pagan Buckeyes as we could corner.

Huffing up a hill, I rounded a bend and spotted my first prospect . . . or perhaps I should say victim. I knew he couldn't get away because his car was pulled over, the hood was up, and he was leaning inside it.

I mustered up a deep breath, sweat dripping from my brow, and said, "Excuse me mister, I have something important to ask you."

The irritated man turned toward me, holding a wrench in his greasy hands.

"What?"

"If you died today would you go to heaven or hell?"

At that moment, I imagined a beautiful light would glow from heaven, with angels singing, "Holy, Holy," and the man would fall on his knees repenting, "I'm headed straight to hell, but I want to go to heaven. What must I do to be saved?"

But it didn't happen that way. Instead, he threatened me with his wrench and told me exactly where to go—and it wasn't heaven.

I made a hasty retreat out of his reach and shouted, "God bless you too, mister!"

Pedaling on down the road and shaking from the adrenaline rush, I counted myself privileged to be persecuted for righteousness' sake.

FLUNKING EVANGELISM BOOT CAMP

As a college sophomore, I volunteered to serve in a parachurch ministry for junior high students. They sent me to evangelism boot camp, which was really a one-day crash course in salvation salesmanship, memorizing Bible verses to use in shoot-outs with sinners.

They insisted the only way lost people would ever find Jesus was for me to memorize a scripted plan and never deviate from it. The approach they used was probably kinder and gentler, but here's a slightly exaggerated version of how I recall it:

Excuse me; I'd like to share the gospel with you:

You are full of the Devil!

Drop the D, it spells *evil* and that's what you are!

Drop the E and that spells *vil* (pronounced "vile"). You are a vile and filthy sinner!

Drop the V and it spells *il* (pronounced "ill"). It makes me ill just to look at you!

Drop the I and all you have left is L. That's where you're headed. Straight to L![1]

That didn't work for me. We were supposed to role-play, demonstrating how well we had mastered the technique. They called me to the front of the class to "convert" our drill instructor. I failed miserably, and Sarge sent me back to my seat, shaking his head in disappointment. I was obviously going to be a youth ministry failure if I couldn't even convert a make-believe pagan.

EVANGELISM EQUALS FAILURE

I once joined the faithful few who didn't know how to say no for "soul-winning night" on Tuesdays and lasted about three weeks. We "Andrews" pounded pavement and poked doorbells, while "Abrahams" stayed behind and prayed. I felt like a flop as an Andrew, wishing all along I had landed, with Aunt Hazel, in the Abraham camp.[2]

These experiences taught me that evangelism equals failure.

I honestly wanted to help others find flourishing faith, but the training I received was actually counterproductive. It made me *less* confident and *more* reluctant to witness. After a few of these distasteful experiences, I concluded that evangelism, like sushi, was not for me.

4
GRACE LEADS
ME HOME

EVERY TRIP I LEARN SOMETHING NEW ABOUT RIVERS, FISH,
AND THE NATURAL WORLD. MOST IMPORTANTLY, I LEARN
SOMETHING NEW ABOUT MYSELF. EVERY ENCOUNTER WITH
THE WATERS OF OUR PLANET DRAWS ME DEEPER INTO
WHO I AM AND WHO I WANT TO BECOME.

Something was missing. I was a professional Christian, raised in a parsonage, went to church three times a week, spent summers at camp, attended a Christian college, married a Christian girl, graduated from seminary, and landed a youth pastor job; but my spiritual life fell woefully short. There's a big difference between serving God and loving him.

I was dry and lukewarm with exterior religion: self-serving at the core with an outer glaze of holiness. Though attempting to cover my soul anemia through busy church activity, Isaiah's lament echoed in my honest moments: "My leanness, my leanness, woe unto me!" (Isa. 24:16 KJV). I was one of those rule-bound Christians who had just enough religion to make myself respectable and miserable.

I actually got away with half-baked spirituality for a while but eventually realized I couldn't do it that way any longer. With growing spiritual discontent, I embarked on an inner pilgrimage to discover what God really wanted for me. This process took several months. During my quest, the word *repent* popped up everywhere. I tried to ignore it. Repenting was for sinners and not for faithful fellows like me. I practiced Mary Poppins Christianity: practically perfect in every way. So repentance seemed unnecessary.

But this message from Jesus repeatedly came to me loud and clear, through reading, music, sermons, and conversations: Repent and believe the gospel.

One day, I felt the nudge to open an old nineteenth-century Methodist theology text, *Elements of Divinity*.[1] I bought it for a quarter at a rummage sale to make my library look impressive, but I had never actually read it. On this day, however, I pulled the book from the shelf and opened it. The chapter title was "Repentance." Finally, God grabbed my attention, as I read the page.

This is my paraphrase of what it said: To find the fullness of Christ, you must (1) see God as he really is, (2) see yourself as you really are, (3) see yourself through God's eyes of grace and mercy, and (4) seek him with all your heart.

That's exactly what I did over the next few weeks.

GRACE WILL LEAD YOU HOME

First, I asked God to help me see him as he really is, and scales fell from my eyes. For the first time in my life, I began to grasp his holiness and majesty. One disadvantage of being raised in a minister's home is over-familiarity with spiritual things. I had viewed Christ as my friend, but failed to understand how high, holy, and mighty God is.

After I captured a glimpse of God's holiness, I saw myself as I really was—not nearly as good and perfect as I previously assumed. Until this experience, I had an inflated view of myself. For instance, I refused to sing the word *wretch* when our congregation sang "Amazing Grace." I thought, "I'm no wretch. That's a horrid word! I'm a decent guy." So I sang *soul* while everybody else sang *wretch*. But my wretchedness surfaced when I saw myself as I really was. In fact, my religious acts were just wretched, self-serving efforts to prop up my image. This took awhile to admit. At first I protested, "God, why are you asking me to repent? I don't have anything to repent of." I was like the lazy housekeeper who kept the lights off so nobody could see the dust. But then God turned on the light, and I saw all sorts of things that needed attention.

Seeing myself through God's eyes of grace and mercy was actually the hardest step because I was so ashamed of being a judgmental, self-righteous hypocrite. It was hard for me to embrace God's grace for myself, recalling something a friend said in a low moment: "I *understand* that he loves the world; I just struggle to believe that he would love *me*."

My quest for peace took me on a journey through arduous interior terrain. Having lived mostly on the surface level, I found such soul-searching extremely painful and frightening. Uncovering all sorts of unholy motives, desires, and ambitions, my heart cried out with the apostle Paul: "O wretched man that I am! Who shall deliver me from the body of this death?" (Rom. 7:24 KJV).

One evening, after a frustrating youth meeting where I harangued the poor students telling them that they were a big disappointment to God, I plopped on the couch and turned on the television to escape. A PBS documentary, *Amazing Grace*, was on. Opera diva Jessye Norman was sharing about the hope she found in her favorite verse of this sacred hymn: "Through many dangers toils and snares I have already come. Tis grace hath brought me safe thus far, and grace will lead me home."[2]

"Deep calls to deep" (Ps. 42:7), and in that moment, something called to the depths of my being—a whisper from heaven, "My grace will lead you home."

MY SANCTUARY EXPERIENCE

Long before dawn the following morning, I drove to the church and entered the sanctuary from a side door. Switching on the light above the piano, I found a hymnal and opened to page 293: "Amazing Grace." I had sung this hymn on countless occasions, but this was the first time I truly embraced it. "Amazing grace! How sweet the sound that saved a wretch like me! I once was lost, but now am found; was blind but now I see."[3]

I knelt at the altar in the empty sanctuary and poured out my heart: "Lord, I'm tired of going through the motions. I need you now and will not settle for lukewarm, halfhearted religion. Please give me the real thing. Take away whatever is unholy in my life and replace it with your love."

I'm not sure how long I prayed, but it was long enough to do business with God. He met me there. It seemed like heaven opened, and God poured out buckets of holy love all over me. My heart overflowed with joy and peace. I felt a tingling, holy energy flowing through me.

The burdens I carried into the church that morning all fell away. My worries and concerns melted in mercy. Resentments turned to forgiveness, and guilt was covered with grace in a beautiful manifestation of God's presence. "Heaven came down and glory filled my soul."[4]

Finally, knowing it was time to rise and face the world, I whispered, "God, if this is real, and not some figment of my imagination, please let me take it with me when I leave." God answered by directing me to a Scripture verse. "May He give you what your heart desires and fulfill your whole purpose (Ps. 20:4 HCSB). I shouted, "Hallelujah!" and bounded from the place a transformed man.

Later that same day I led someone to Christ for the first time. Until then I never considered myself an evangelist. I always shrank back from such encounters. But now that I was juiced with Jesus, he gave me an opportunity to share his love.

Someone knocked at my office door. I was surprised to find Brenda, a former youth group member, standing there. She had been missing from church for months. "I don't know why I'm here," she stammered, "I was walking by the church just now and something made me turn and knock at your door."

"I know exactly why you're here!" I replied. "Let me tell you what Jesus did for me this morning!"

As I recounted my experience, Brenda wept. "I need that too. Can you help me find it?"

There in my office Brenda surrendered her life to Christ. That day I began to understand that evangelism is not some grim duty, but rather a beautiful gift that comes from overflowing love.

5
ICH-THEOLOGY

JESUS, PRICELESS TREASURE, SOURCE OF PUREST
PLEASURE, TRUEST FRIEND TO ME.

—JOHANN FRANCK

Jesus himself is the gift, the greatest treasure the world has ever seen. He is our ultimate purple fish!

Ichthyology is the study of fish. It comes from the Greek word *ichthus*, which became a symbol for Jesus (the letters representing "Jesus Christ God's Son Savior").

The early church father Tertullian said, "But we little fish, like our Fish [*ichthus*] Jesus Christ, are born in water, and it is only by remaining in water that we are safe."[1] I suppose you could call that "Ich-theology."[2]

BIG FISH

Hayward, Wisconsin, is home of the big fish. Our most notable landmark is a three-story structure shaped like a musky. Tourists pay money to climb the staircase inside and stand in the big fish mouth. (I've performed two weddings in the musky mouth.) This tourist attraction on the Freshwater Fishing Hall of Fame grounds symbolizes the glorious fishing culture of Hayward. Our world-record muskies are legendary.[3] Anglers come from everywhere in search of the elusive pike. Landing a fifty-inch musky, the fish of ten thousand casts, is a fisherman's greatest accomplishment.

THE MESSIAH MYSTIQUE

The world's greatest musky historian, Larry Ramsell, told me that once you get a strike, you'll have the fever for life. He calls it the "muskie mystique."[4] Quite a few of my up-north buddies have caught this bug and, as far as I know, it's incurable.

When you have a genuine Christ encounter, you will get Jesus fever for the rest of your life: the "Messiah mystique." Once he strikes your soul, you're changed forever. I know. It happened to me.

THE GOSPEL IS A PERSON

The Christian gospel is a person, not a belief system or religious practice. It is neither a code of conduct nor a sectarian membership, but rather a real relationship with a living person. Truth is a treasure with nail holes in his hands.

Jesus is the pearl of great price and the treasure in the field. He is worth everything, and without him, you have nothing. When you find purple-fish Jesus, you've found all you need.

THE BEST FRIEND I EVER HAD

"Something's seriously wrong with Bert. He's shut down and won't respond to anybody. Maybe you can get through to him."

The concerned nurse called to see if I could swing by the hospital to visit the eccentric octogenarian. Since I shared responsibility for his hospitalization, she figured I should at least try to get him to cooperate.

Bert lived off the land like a hermit, talked with animals like Dr. Doolittle, composed over a thousand hymns like Charles Wesley, and avoided bathing like Pig-Pen. He also avoided pills, physicians, and all manner of medical attention except for his own homeopathic concoctions.

For nearly nine decades, his homemade cures worked fairly well, but a bad case of pneumonia combined with an infection brought him near death's door. When I showed up at his shack for a pastoral visit and saw his deteriorating condition, I called 9-1-1.

Bert was ticked when the EMTs arrived, loaded him in an ambulance, and whisked him to Hayward Hospital, but he didn't have the energy to fight. So he protested his "incarceration" by shutting down and not responding to anyone.

Bert was flat on his back with eyes closed and hands folded when I entered the hospital room on the third day of his protest.

"Bert, how are you feeling today?"

No response.

"I hear you aren't talking to anybody."

Silence.

"Can I read a passage of Scripture?"

Nothing.

I tried the environment, religion, and politics. Normally, he would rant for an hour whenever any of those subjects came up.

Still no response.

I said a quick prayer and turned to leave but was stopped by a strong impression to sing "What a Friend We Have in Jesus." At first, I hesitated. I didn't want anyone to hear me. What if my crooning carried down the hall? What if a nurse showed up during my performance? But in obedience to the Spirit, I turned back to Bert and told him I was going to sing a hymn before departing.

"What a friend we have in Jesus, all our sins and griefs to bear. What a privilege to carry everything to God in prayer."[5]

Bert's eyes remained closed as I sang, but his face broke into a huge smile. He raised one arm, pointed his bony finger toward heaven and said, "Jesus . . . is my strength. Jesus . . . is my song. Jesus . . . is my salvation. Jesus is the best friend I ever had!"

When Bert remembered what a great treasure he had in Jesus, the sun broke through and chased away the clouds. "Satisfy us in the morning with your unfailing love, that we may sing for joy and be glad all our days" (Ps. 90:14).

6
TREASURING
THE
TREASURE

I MAY WONDER WHAT KIND OF MISSION GOD HAS
FOR ME, WHEN I SHOULD ASK WHAT KIND OF
ME GOD WANTS FOR HIS MISSION.

—CHRISTOPHER J. H. WRIGHT

Jesus, our purple fish, is certainly worth treasuring. His love flows beyond measure or imagination. As hymnist Isaac Watts put it, "Love so amazing, so divine, demands my soul, my life, my all."[1]

We treasure the Treasure through worship (the journey upward), holiness (the journey inward), and mission (the journey outward).[2]

WORSHIP: THE JOURNEY UPWARD

The English word *worship* is actually a contraction of *worth-ship*: to honor what is honorable, or treasuring the treasure.

Worship is not a music genre or religious liturgy. It is not a Sunday morning event. Rather, it is a heart flowing with reverent love for Christ. As Mark Batterson stated, "Singing is something you do with your voice. Worship is something you do with your heart."[3]

Worship cultivates wonder, recognizing God's nearness.

HOLINESS: THE JOURNEY INWARD

Holiness is worship in action. It means living in holy love with "the gaze of the soul" upon Christ rather than ourselves or our circumstances.[4] It requires total devotion without reservation. You can't be full of Jesus when you're full of other things.

Holiness reflects our love for our Savior. If we love him, we will desire what he desires, love what he loves, and do what he wants. You please the one you love most.

Our holiness comes from Christ within, not from ourselves. "But we have this treasure in jars of clay to show that this all-surpassing power is from God and not from us" (2 Cor. 4:7). Homemade holiness is only self-righteousness in disguise.

Before pointing the way for others, we need to get the point ourselves.

Richard Baxter, vicar of Kidderminster, penned the following advice to pastors: "Take heed, therefore, to ourselves first, that you be that which you persuade your hearers to be, and believe that which you persuade them to believe, and heartily entertain that Savior whom you offer to them."[5]

MISSION: THE JOURNEY OUTWARD

We cannot share what we do not have. Unless our mission flows from worship and holiness, we're just hypocrites playing silly religious games.

True evangelism means pouring out genuine love for others, and this comes from the overflow. The quality of our love for people hangs entirely on our love for Christ, as singleness of intent combines with wideness of spirit.

Jesus is the source, the end, and the means of all worship, holiness, and mission. He does not ask us to do things for him, but rather with and through him. There's joy in the journey when Jesus leads the way.

7
EUANGELION:
BETTER THAN GREAT NEWS

FISHING IS MUCH MORE THAN FISH.

—HERBERT HOOVER

The Greek word for gospel, *euangelion*, means good news, though, quite frankly, that's an understatement. Ancient Romans used it for fabulous announcements, such as a royal birth or military conquest. It's actually better than great news. It's better-than-you-ever-imagined-jump-up-and-down-and-shout-yippee news. It's better than the best news you have ever received.

THE GROCERY CONTEST

We've had a few whooping, red-letter euangelion experiences at the Wilson home over the years, such as when the Packers won the Super Bowl and the time Uncle Sam and Aunt Linda treated our whole gang to a week at Disneyworld.

The Marketplace Grocery contest, however, tops them all.

Living on a one-income pastor's salary was challenging. Growing boys eat a lot. My wife, Cathy, struggled with increased pressure on our food budget.

Then one day, Marketplace Grocery announced a drawing for a free year's supply of groceries. Cathy submitted her name and decided to pray to win. I rolled my eyes when she did that. It reminded me of the people who pray to win the lottery. So far, none of those prayers have availed (that I know of at least). So when Cathy started praying to win the grocery lotto, I made a joke of it.

Drawing day happened to be on Sunday. Our family sat at the breakfast table before church, and Cathy said grace: "Dear Lord, I just want to remind you that today's the grocery drawing. We sure could use them, and if it's your will, it would be wonderful if we won."

As soon as she said "Amen," I took advantage of this teaching moment and rebuked her right in front of the kids: "Now, Honey, that's not the way we're supposed to pray. It's not proper to ask God for free stuff like that. God doesn't work that way—and even if he did, what would that teach our kids? That you can get something for nothing!"

"Well, I disagree," Cathy responded. "First, I'm not demanding that God do this. I'm just asking, and if he says no, I'm fine with that. And second, if we happened to win, it would teach our children that God loves us and that he hears and answers our prayers."

The kids all sided with her: "Yeah, Dad! You should listen to Mom."

I left for church in a huff.

During the worship service, I was giving announcements when the office phone rang. One of our ushers answered and then bounded up the middle aisle with a goofy grin on his face, waving a little piece of paper.

It was a note saying, "Marketplace Grocery just called. Your family won the groceries!"

Well, this was a thrilling announcement! I shared the news with my congregation, and they cheered, delighted that it was their poor preacher, rather than some wealthy tourist from Minnesota who had hit the jackpot.

It sure was hard to preach with gravitas that Sunday, knowing that our family had just won a year's supply of groceries.

After church, we arrived home and found our answering machine blinking. The store manager had called our house before dialing the church. "Hello, this is Jon from Marketplace.

Congratulations Cathy Wilson, you just won the groceries! Come to the store as soon as you can to claim your prize!"

All seven of us held hands in a circle, jumped up and down, and shouted with glee, "We won the groceries! We won the groceries! We won the groceries!"

Then, one of our boys said, "Hit it again, Dad!"

So, I hit the button, and we heard the message all over again, and then repeated the jumping and shouting exercise. We did that four times, before we finally piled into the van and headed to the store.

When we arrived at Marketplace, they were waiting for us, holding a big check with Cathy's name on it. Terrell, the omnipresent photographer from the *Sawyer County Record* showed up to cover the event.

He leaned toward my son, Luke, who was five, and said, "It must be wonderful for your family to win all these groceries."

"Yeah," Luke replied before I could cover his mouth. "Mom prayed that we would win them, but Dad didn't believe it could happen."

Cathy smiled while I squirmed.

The delight of that moment, relived and retold around the Wilson table, is but a tiny taste of the great euangelion: the gospel of Jesus.

REMEMBER AGAIN

The gospel is better than the best news you've ever received. Anyone who's experienced it personally knows the majesty of the moment. Yet for some strange reason, we tend to forget. Maybe it would be a good idea to revisit and experience again "the hour we first believed."

Remember the joy of your salvation. Remember the freedom of forgiveness. Go back and taste grace again for the first time. Renew your first love. It's better than great news.

8
LOST TREASURES

DEFINE YOURSELF RADICALLY AS ONE BELOVED BY GOD.
THIS IS THE TRUE SELF. EVERY OTHER IDENTITY IS ILLU-
SION.

—BRENNAN MANNING

Jesus is our euangelion—better than great news. He is our ultimate purple fish—the greatest treasure the world has ever seen.

This leads us to an important question: What does Jesus treasure? What matters most to him? People! More than anything else in the universe, Jesus treasures people, and that includes you and me. We are his purple fish. Christ cared enough to come rescue us personally. As Bishop Festo Kivengere said, "God is love in action—love rushing on a rescue mission."[1]

LOST CAUSES

Perhaps it would be good to rethink how we view those who seem far from Christ. We write off people too quickly as lost causes when we ought to consider them lost treasures instead.

Jesus came to redeem and restore people—particularly lost, broken, hurting people. This includes us all because everyone is lost, broken, and hurting in one aspect or another. We're a bunch of dinged-up wrecks.

Jesus rectifies what we've wrecked, however, bringing beauty from brokenness and grace from disgrace. Rumi, the Afghan poet, observed, "Where there is ruin, there is hope for a treasure."[2] Lost people, then, are lost treasures and we should value them as such.

Don't hide your brokenness. Give it to God. Put it in his hands. Perhaps you will find a treasure there. Ask Christ to patch the holes and see what he does. When we bring our broken pieces to God, he puts them together again in a beautiful new way. "I am the LORD, who heals you" (Ex. 15:26). God invites us to bring our emptiness and brokenness to him and he will make us whole again. His holiness transforms our hole-i-ness into whole-i-ness.

HEALTHY ON THE INSIDE

Sandy was visibly upset when she approached me after church one Sunday. "I have an urgent prayer request. My friend Pam was in a terrible car accident last night. She's in intensive care at St. Mary's with a broken neck. It's uncertain whether she will ever walk again." Then Sandy added, "Ironically, she was planning to come to church with me this morning, and now this happened."

That afternoon, I made the long trek to Duluth to visit Sandy's friend.

Pam, strapped and bolted in a Stryker frame, recognized me immediately as I entered her room: "I was going to visit your church this morning."

"Well, I came to visit you instead."

We had a deep, meaningful conversation and concluded with prayer. I could tell her heart was especially tender toward spiritual things.

As I headed toward the door, she said, "Don't be surprised when I walk into your worship service some Sunday."

Several months later, I was preaching, when the sanctuary door opened and Pam entered. After extensive therapy, she had learned to walk again. She hobbled down the center aisle and sat near the front. I stopped mid-sermon to explain the miracle we had just witnessed, and the congregation gave Pam a standing ovation. God's message that morning was far better than the one I had prepared.

Pam attended regularly after that, discovering a rich and vibrant faith. It was exciting to see her grow. We baptized Pam on the one-year anniversary of her accident. On the shore of Little Round Lake, before stepping into the water, Pam gave the following testimony: "A year and a day ago, I was healthy on the outside, but unhealthy on the inside. An accident left me not-so-healthy on the outside. But thank God, I'm healthy on the inside. I'd rather have this than that any day."

BEAUTY FROM BROKENNESS

A few years ago, I preached from Psalm 147:3: "He heals the brokenhearted and binds up their wounds." My theme that Sunday was how God puts broken pieces back together in a new creation more beautiful than the first. To illustrate, I smashed several ceramic floor tiles into fragments with a hammer.

"We are broken by disappointment." Wham!

"Broken by grief." Wham!

"Broken by rejection, sin, and suffering." Wham, wham, wham!

Then I took the shards and handed them to Joan, a gifted artist, who stepped onto the platform behind me.

While I finished preaching, Joan created a mosaic, transforming the shards into a beautiful piece of art. Joan wept as she literally brought beauty from brokenness, a testimony of God's redemptive work in her own life.

At the end of the service, when she showed us her masterpiece, everybody said, "That's me!"

The mosaic now hangs in our church foyer, reminding us that lost people are God's lost treasures, and mending broken lives is his specialty.

9
A STORY CALLED REDEMPTION

I'M FISHING FOR MEN WITH A CERTAIN KIND OF BAIT,
AND THE BAIT THAT I AM OFFERING IS NOT A CANDY; IT'S
A VERY SPECIFIC THING THAT I'M OFFERING, WHICH IS
A DEEP GOSPEL AND A DEEP CONVERSION.

—LARRY NORMAN

I love learning more about my ancestry. Cathy comes from a long line of refined professionals, preachers, and educators. My roots go back to hillbillies, rabble-rousers, and moonshiners.

Digging up dead relatives one evening, I was thrilled to stumble upon a respectable Wilson.

"Guess what?" I said to Cathy. "My oldest ancestor was a ship captain!"

"Must have been a pirate."

That burst my bubble.

"Arrg! You'll walk the plank for insulting grandpappy like that!"

I used to share my latest genealogical gems with house guests, but they didn't seem to appreciate it much. Not everybody is fascinated by the fact that my great-great-grandad died from diarrhea or that great-grandma's aunt survived the 1874 grasshopper plague.

Those things intrigue me, because they are personal. My ancestors are a part of my story, and I am a part of theirs. When it's personal, it's interesting.

IN A BIGGER STORY

The gospel is the most interesting story ever because it's so personal. God personally steps into our stories and, even better, invites us to step into his.

God works everywhere, doing wonderful acts in this sweeping drama called life. As Gerard Manley Hopkins said, "Christ plays in ten thousand places."[1] He invites us to come join him in this creative play. How enthralling! This is much bigger than simply asking Jesus into our hearts. Rather, it is us joining with Jesus and following his script, which is richer and fuller than anything we could possibly create on our own.

In God's grand redemption story, we humans are created for good, broken by sin, redeemed by grace, and sent to bless and heal.

CREATED FOR GOOD

God made people in his image (Gen. 1:26), and we all reflect that in one way or another. Every good and wonderful part of being human connects directly to this truth. God is at work within us, even when we're unaware of it.

The love of marriage, joys of childhood, and peace of home are all snippets of Eden, pointing to our original creation.

BROKEN BY SIN

However, as a result of Eden's fall (Gen. 3), we all are broken by sin. Sin is our separation from God, our human tendency to mess things up.

After Adam and Eve sinned by eating from the wrong tree, they were ashamed, hid, and covered themselves with fig leaves. Sons of Adam and daughters of Eve have faked it with fig leaves ever sense. Forbidden fruit makes bad jam. Guilt is bitter. Shame is sour.

From Genesis 3 onward, the Bible deals with the guilt and shame problem.

Only one thing eliminates guilt: justice. When a crime is committed, payment must be made for justice to prevail. This is the point of all religious sacrificial systems, including those in the Old Testament. Wrongdoing calls for appeasement. Many primitive societies practiced animal and even human sacrifice because humans innately know some sort of atonement must be made to assuage guilt. "Without the shedding of blood, there is no forgiveness" (Heb. 9:22). The Old Testament calls for the blood of sheep and bulls to be spilt as a personal sacrifice for sin, demonstrating the high price of justice. As a Jewish man brought his sacrifice for slaughter, he was to think, "This animal should be me."

Justice takes care of guilt but does not eliminate shame. Even when the dues are paid and atonement is made, shame still remains. Only one thing removes shame: pure, unconditional love.

REDEEMED BY GRACE

This is the heart of the gospel—euangelion. Jesus, the Lamb of God, died on the cross to take away both guilt and shame. His blood was spilled as a sacrifice for sin—and that takes away our guilt. He poured out pure, unconditional love on the cross—and that removes our shame. "But God demonstrates his own love for us in this: While we were still sinners, Christ died for us

(Rom. 5:8). We no longer need to live in the bondage of guilt or the shadow of shame. Christ died for all and sets us free.

Through grace, God makes wrong things right, restoring the created order. Jesus steps personally into our space and invites us to swap stories. The adventure really begins when we trade our story for his.

SENT TO BLESS AND HEAL

Redeemed people are sent on a redemption mission. Evangelism is simply how followers of Jesus interact with the world. It's not a program or a project; it's a life.

Since I've been blessed, I will be a blessing. Since I have been healed, I will bring healing. Since I have been saved, I will serve.

Personal salvation means joining heaven's earthly mission as "one beggar telling another beggar where to find bread."[2]

10
MENDING
FOR
SENDING

THE FIRST MEN THAT OUR SAVIOR DEAR DID CHOOSE TO
WAIT UPON HIM HERE, BLEST FISHERS WERE; AND FISH
THE LAST FOOD WAS,
THAT HE ON EARTH DID TASTE: I THEREFORE STRIVE TO
FOLLOW THOSE, WHOM HE TO FOLLOW HIM HATH
CHOSE.

We were made for a mission. God pours blessing into our lives, so we can turn around and bless others. Jesus said, "As the Father has sent me, I am sending you" (John 20:21).

FOUR FISH, FOUR FISHERMEN

Jesus, went to the lake on a purple fish fishing trip one day and caught four keepers: Peter, Andrew, James, and John. Isn't that ironic? Jesus, the ultimate purple fish, became the fisherman, and the fishermen became the fish. He prized them as great treasures. What a catch!

Then, Jesus turned it upside down again. He took these fishermen fish, cleaned them up, and gave them a new mission to be "fishers of men" (Matt. 4:19 NIV84).

Jesus practices catch and release. He fishes for us then sends us fishing. He seeks us to save us, and mends us to send us.

SEEKING FOR SAVING

Finding Jesus is not a Where's Waldo puzzle. It's not that Jesus is lost and we're searching for him. We're the lost ones, and he is looking for us. Christ seeking the lost is painted poignantly in Luke 15 in parables of the lost sheep, the lost coin, and the lost son. Bill Hybels distilled these stories into three observations:

- Something of great value was missing.
- That which was missing was important enough to warrant an all-out search.
- Retrieval resulted in great rejoicing.[1]

Jesus seeks us to save us from our sins, ourselves, and our circumstances.

MENDING FOR SENDING

Being caught in Christ's salvation net is only the first step. Along with his love, he brings healing grace for our inner wounds and repairs the damage from our brokenness. God loves us too much to waste our painful experiences. He salvages our shame and redeems our regrets. The place of great *pain* becomes the place of great *gain*. When Jesus steps in, his healing touch changes the entire outcome. Jesus mends us to send us—joining him in the greatest adventure on earth. Salvation joy overflows. We can't help but share this with others.

Christ began with the disciples with "Come and follow me" (see John 1:39), and in the end, wrapped it up with "Go and tell others" (see Mark 16:15). Wherever Jesus finds us, he calls us to follow him, and then go into the world, sharing his love.

MISSIONARIES IN THE MAKING

Every broken life has potential for mission. There's a message in every mess. Can you grasp that? If so, it will change the way you see people. Everyone you meet, regardless of how wretched their life may seem, is a missionary in the making.

Understanding this transformed the way I view certain ministry responsibilities. For instance, instead of seeing marriage counseling as an energy drain, I consider distressed couples as marriage missionaries in the making. They don't know it yet, but when God restores their relationship, they will be equipped to help others in marital conflict.

When refereeing a dispute, I picture both parties as future ambassadors of peace and conflict resolution.

When needy neighbors seek financial assistance, I try to look beneath the surface to their inner struggle, and treat them as potential missionaries of abundance and generosity.

I admit, this doesn't always work. Marriages still blow up, people still squabble, and chronic poverty persists. However, like Jesus, I choose to look for potential and dig deeper to find buried treasure.

Even if their situation doesn't improve, my attitude does, and that keeps the hope door open for all of us. "If you change how you see people," said Rick Warren, "the people you see will change."[2]

FRANK, THE FISH COUNTER

My biologist buddy, Frank, worked for the Department of Natural Resources, monitoring fish populations in area lakes. When conducting fish counts, he shocked the water, and stunned fish floated to the surface. I always figured it would be fun to go zap fishing with Frank and his stun-gun boat.

One May, Frank was severely injured in a terrible traffic accident. While hospitalized far from home, Frank experienced a spiritual stunning. God zapped him and gave him a new mission.

"I would not be arrogant enough to compare my experience with St. Paul's getting knocked off his donkey on the way to Damascus," Frank said. "I just got knocked off my Subaru on the way to Indiana."

Frank the fish counter was a purple fish who counted with God.

After Frank recovered from his injuries, he retired and launched a community mentoring program called Sons and Daughters of Zebedee, combining three great loves: God, fishing, and children.

Mending leads to sending and that brings great fulfillment. Recently, I overheard Frank explain his new vocation: "I'm fishin' with a mission now."

11
TREASURE BEARERS, TREASURE SEEKERS

SOMETHING HIDDEN. GO AND FIND IT. GO AND LOOK BEYOND THE RANGES—SOMETHING LOST BEHIND THE RANGES. LOST AND WAITING FOR YOU. GO!

—RUDYARD KIPLING

The fullness of holy love overflows naturally to others. "God wants us to *have* an encounter, so that we *become* an encounter, so that *others* can have an encounter," stated spiritual treasure hunter, Kevin Dedmon.[1]

In other words, we get to carry Jesus, the world's greatest treasure, to the ones he prizes most. What a privilege that Jesus would invite us on this adventure of seeking lost treasures.

BAPTISM IN THE ICU

One day I received a phone call from a woman who asked if I would come to the hospital. Her dying mother wanted to be baptized. I agreed and made the journey, praying all the way.

Arriving at the intensive care unit, I found the lady in bed. Wires were hooked up everywhere. Three grown daughters and one son surrounded her.

I asked, "Are you seeking peace with God?"

"Yes! That's exactly what I need."

Gently, I shared the gospel, and she opened her heart to Jesus. It was beautiful. After that, I took some bedside ice water and baptized her. Usually, I dunk converts in the lake, but a sprinkling of holy ice water does the trick in intensive care units.

In that moving moment, the daughter who had called me said, "Can you do it for me too?" So I prayed with her to receive Christ and baptized her with holy ice water. The second daughter said, "How about me?" So we prayed, and I baptized her with the ice water too. Then the third daughter said, "Count me in!" So I did the same thing for her.

Finally the son, a gruff outdoorsman in camo, grunted, "Well, I suppose I need it too." So he also received prayer and the holy ice water baptism.

It was a glorious occasion. We hugged each other, and I nearly floated from that hospital room, thanking God for allowing me to carry the treasure to these precious souls.

One of the daughters ran down the hall after me, interrupting my bliss. "Wait, Pastor! Wait a minute!" She fumbled in her purse, pulled out a five dollar bill, and said, "Here, go have a beer on me."

Oh, what an infinite joy to carry the treasure to people who need it so desperately! Nothing compares with it. Isn't it great that God allows us to tag along on such delightful adventures?

THE GREAT MINNOW EVACUATION

Several years ago, eight-year-old Hannah and I went on a dad and daughter date, hiking the dry bed of Smith Creek. Due to a summer drought, the creek had evaporated into a crusty maze of cracked soil, dry rocks, and broken branches. We walked where the water used to be.

Rounding a bend, Hannah pointed and shouted, "Look, Daddy! Minnows!"

Sure enough, a small mud puddle, not more than three feet in diameter, bubbled with life. The last of the Smith Creek minnows desperately flopped in a small, shrinking sanctuary.

"We have to do something, Daddy, or they're going to die!" Hannah urged.

"I'm sure they'll be fine."

"No, they won't be fine, Daddy. Can't you see they need our help? Their lives are in our hands! We have to save them. Please?"

How could I refuse that?

We dashed home and returned, armed with a small goldfish net and a super-size Hardee's cup. We were on a mission. Together, we scooped the little fish from the puddle one at a time. In a half hour of scooping, we rescued all nineteen minnows. Then it was time to evacuate.

Now, I realize there's a Wisconsin law against transporting minnows from one body of water to another, but desperate times call for desperate measures, even civil disobedience.

Quickly, we sped to the Namekagon River, where Hannah gently released the little critters one at a time, with words of encouragement: "Good-bye fishy. Have a nice life."

"We saved them all, Daddy," Hannah beamed on our way home. "We saved them all! I like this kind of fishing."

PART 2

FISHING TIPS
AND
TREASURE MAPS

MAY THE HOLES IN YOUR NET BE NO LARGER
THAN THE FISH IN IT.

—IRISH BLESSING

THROW YOUR NET ON THE RIGHT SIDE OF THE
BOAT AND YOU WILL FIND SOME.

—JOHN 21:6

12

THE BEST WAY

TO

SHARE YOUR FAITH

GOING FISHING IS A STATEMENT OF FAITH.

—ANONYMOUS

Can you come visit Harold?" the young woman pleaded. "He's dying of cancer."

Harold was an ex-convict who had lived a violent, godless life.

"Of course, Harold probably won't receive you well," she continued. "He's likely to cuss up a storm and kick you out. He's done that already with a few hospice workers, but a visit from you might be good for him."

I agreed to go and invited my friend, Randy, to come along as my bouncer. I brought my Bible, anointing oil, and a prayer shawl.

The young lady met us at the door of Harold's bungalow. "I told him you're coming, but he's shut down and won't communicate. I'm afraid you won't get anywhere."

In the living room, frail Harold sat hunched on the couch in his pajamas. He didn't look up. "Harold, I'm Pastor Mark from the Wesleyan church, and this is Randy. We came to encourage you today."

No response from Harold.

"I brought a gift for you Harold. It's a prayer shawl. Some wonderful women in our congregation make these, and while they knit, they pray for the ones who will receive them. Would it be alright if I placed the shawl over your shoulders and prayed for you?"

Harold didn't say anything. He just sat there. Since he didn't say no, I took it as a yes. Placing the soft shawl over his shoulders, I said, "Harold, if you don't mind, I'd love to share some Scripture and anoint you with oil. Then we'll pray."

Still no response, so I moved forward.

I opened my black leather Bible to Psalm 23, handed it to Randy, then gave the bottle of anointing oil to Harold's friend. "I would like for you to anoint Harold when Randy reads the part that says, 'You anoint my head with oil; my cup overflows'" (v. 5).

She seemed honored, though a bit nervous about doing it right. I gave her simple instructions, and she was ready to go.

Harold didn't look up or say anything.

Randy read Psalm 23 with passion, and as he got to the fifth verse, the young lady reached forward tenderly, making a cross on Harold's forehead. Then I prayed.

Harold needed some faith, so I loaned him mine. I prayed, on Harold's behalf, for salvation, with as much faith as I could muster. "Harold needs you, Lord. Please come right now and help him." I asked God to forgive and cleanse all his sins. I prayed for Harold to be completely enfolded in God's gracious love and peace. I concluded by thanking God for the depth and width of his mercy.

When I said amen, Randy whispered, "Look."

A tear trickled down Harold's wrinkled cheek. He didn't say a word, but that tear testified to something.

I remembered Philip Yancey's observation, "Grace, like water, flows to the lowest part."[1]

Two days later, Harold died. The family called to make funeral arrangements. "Everything changed after you came," they said. "He settled into a deep peace and wasn't agitated any longer. It was exactly what Harold needed. And here's the most amazing thing. That prayer shawl you gave him? He held it tightly and wouldn't let go. Even when we tried to take it from him, he just clung to it like a life preserver, and so it stayed wrapped over his shoulders till the moment he died."

I was astounded. When this man, who lived so far from God, passed away, he was wrapped in holy love.

Jesus is a friend of sinners. He is not willing that any should perish and takes great measures to grant grace to needy souls.

The best way to share your faith is to loan it to someone who needs it.

"Come, every soul by sin oppressed; there's mercy with the Lord, and he will surely give you rest by trusting in his Word."[2]

13
TWO KINDS
OF
FISHING

THE CHARM OF FISHING IS THAT IT IS THE PURSUIT
OF WHAT IS ELUSIVE BUT ATTAINABLE,
A PERPETUAL SERIES OF OCCASIONS FOR HOPE.

—JOHN BUCHAN

Standing in line to buy worms at Pastika's Bait Shop, I ran into
my buddy, Kenny. He carried a bucket containing a big fish.

"Wow, Kenny, what a nice fish! Where did you get it?"

"Right here," he grinned, "I just bought it. It's my bait."

My worms suddenly felt very small.

In an attempt to console me, Kenny added, "But if I don't
catch a musky, I'll just fry this fellow for dinner."

That day, I realized there are two kinds of fishing.

There are also two different approaches to sharing the gospel: the pearl merchant and the treasure hunter.[1]

PEARL MERCHANT: I HAVE SOMETHING YOU NEED

The pearl merchant says, "I have something great and you need it." If the person on the receiving end is in the market for pearls, then this approach works splendidly. After all, everybody does better when they discover the pearl of great price (see Matt. 13:45–46). People certainly need Jesus, and knowing him is the greatest joy on earth.

When our hearts are captivated by grace, we naturally want to share Christ with others. However, unrestrained enthusiasm in pushing pearls often backfires and pushes people away.

One pearl merchant pitfall is *condescension*—an attitude of superiority: "I have the answer, and you are clueless." In extreme cases, sidewalk evangelists blast messages of repentance through bullhorns and wonder why nobody responds. We all recoil from those who convey a condescending attitude and immediately seek an exit strategy.

Another pitfall is *coercion*. Some pearl merchant evangelists are mean-spirited. They're the ones who give evangelism a bad name, suffering from what B. T. Roberts called "a warring holiness."[2] These folks bulldoze and won't take no for an answer:

"You're going to have it whether you want it or not." Evangelism without loving-kindness is brutal coercion. I'm pretty sure Jesus has an anti-bullying policy for his children.

During my youth pastor days, Victor, a varsity football lineman, came to youth group with a glowing report. "Guess what? I led six freshmen to Jesus this week!"

"Wow, that's great Victor," I replied. "How did you do it?"

"Simple," he explained. "I caught them in the hallway, grabbed them by the collar, slammed them into the locker, and asked if they'd rather have Jesus or a knuckle sandwich."

Of course, all the freshmen said they would rather have Jesus.

TREASURE HUNTER: YOU ARE VALUABLE

The second approach is more along this line: "Here you are! I've been looking for you!" This is how Jesus loves the lost. He seeks them out and reveals their true worth. Compassion always leads the way.

One April afternoon, our family combed the Lake Superior North Shore in search of agates.

"Here's one, Dad," Wes said from behind me. "You just stepped on it—and look, there are more."

Sure enough, agates were strewn across the rocky beach, but they seemed so ordinary, I trampled on them. I was searching for something with more sparkle and zing. Thankfully, Wes walked with a different set of eyes. On the shoreline, buried in dust, the agates appeared insignificant. However, when we found one, dipped it in water and held it to the sunlight, it shone like a jewel.

Our job, as treasure hunters, is to look again—look beyond the ordinary. "The sacred gems are scattered at the head of every street" (Lam. 4:1 NIV84). Lost treasures are everywhere.

Dip them in God's grace, lift them to the Sun of Righteousness, and they will gleam. Seek, and you shall find.

14
PRAY
THEM IN

MANY FISHERMEN PRAY IN TIMES OF STRESS AND
I KNOW I FEEL NEARER TO GOD AND MORE RELIGIOUS
WHEN FIGHTING FISH THAN AT ANY OTHER TIME.

—S. KIP HARRINGTON

Prayer is the most powerful resource we have in sharing the gospel. When interceding for others, we are literally touching heaven on their behalf. It's supernatural business—a cooperation between the human and divine. "Prayer," said Wesley Duewel, "is the supreme way to be workers together with God."[1]

PRAYER OPENS THE WAY

When we pray, God opens a way. I don't understand how it works, but I know that it does. Ed Silvoso said, "Prayer evangelism is talking to God about our neighbors before we talk to our neighbors about God."[2] Praying for others is the most loving act you can perform for them.

The answer may not come right away, but don't give up. Keep on praying. After all, your prayers are eternal and gain compound interest in heaven. Persistent prayer provides a path of hope to loved ones who are lost without Christ. It will accomplish much more than arguing and pressuring. Eventually, the answer will come if you do not lose heart.

THE SILVERTHORN RESURRECTION

On the day of our annual church picnic and baptism at Silverthorn Lake, Don, who was on the list to be immersed, approached me. He had experienced a difficult life, filled with pain, sorrow, and regret, but recently found a new faith in Christ.

"I'm not sure if I can be baptized today."

"Why not, Don?"

"Thirty years ago, my brother drowned while swimming in Silverthorn. It's a place of death and horror for me. I've stayed far away ever since."

"Well, Don, we can arrange for you to be baptized someplace else."

"No, I need to do this. It's important, but bad memories make this hard. Do you have a cross I can hold when you dunk me under water?"

A visitor from Indiana happened to bring a box of small hand-carved crosses that very morning. God knew exactly what Don needed and provided it just in time, through our Hoosier friend.

"Yes, I have a cross for you, Don, sent from heaven, just for this occasion. We're going to do this together, and God is going to help us."

Don blew out a deep breath and said, "Yes, God help us."

On the shore of Silverthorn, Don told the crowd about his brother's death, his struggles, and his desire to follow Jesus. He thanked God for restoring his faith, asked for the prayers of the people, then stepped into the water. Don literally shook with dread before we plunged him beneath the surface, but he emerged with renewed courage and hope.

His mother rushed to the shoreline in sheer joy to meet her dripping son. After a warm embrace, she asked to speak.

"I have prayed many years for this day! For those parents who have been praying earnestly for your prodigal children—never give up! Keep on praying! Keep on believing! God's going to answer someday."

Faithful prayer wins the victory.

That August afternoon, Silverthorn Lake was transformed from a place of death to resurrection as a couple hundred folks on earth joined the multitudes in heaven, rejoicing over a sinner who had finally been prayed home.

15
HONOR
THE
PROCESS

YOU CANNOT, OF COURSE, FISH FOR BIG CARP IN
HALF A DAY. IT TAKES A MONTH.

—H. T. SHERINGHAM

Not everybody comes to Christ the same way. For some, it's a dramatic, overnight transformation. But more often, the redemption road is a long, winding pilgrimage.

SHEPHERDS AND WISE MEN

The Christmas story captures this well.

Bethlehem shepherds hunkered around a nighttime campfire, minding their own business, when an angel of the Lord came down and glory shone around (see Luke 2:9). Amazed, they instantly dropped everything and ran to the manger.

Some spiritual breakthroughs are like that.

For instance, my friend Ken received instantaneous healing and deliverance from an alcohol addiction that had nearly killed him. Afterwards, when I recommended a 12-step recovery program, he declined. "For me, it was a one-step program—straight to Jesus." Though certainly recognizing the tremendous value of 12-step programs, I didn't argue with Ken. How could I dispute his personal healing experience?

More often, people come to Christ by the way of the magi who pondered the eastern star from afar, then began their long voyage to Bethlehem. They had deep questions and searched for answers. Eventually, the journey brought them to Jesus—just like the shepherds.

We don't all find Jesus in the same way, and not everybody is at the same place. We must meet them where they are, rather than where we wish they'd be. There is a process to conversion. We're all at different points along the faith continuum.[1]

It is helpful to understand and accept people where they are spiritually. Your job as an evangelist is not to "convert" people, but to love and bless them, sensitively nudging them toward Jesus. God will do the converting if we are faithful and patient in our loving. On average, it takes 7.6 spiritual conversations before seekers open their lives to Christ.[2] Each of those conversations is equally important.

One farmer plants seeds, another pulls weeds, and a third reaps the harvest. They are all doing the same work. In childbirth, the one who gives prenatal care is as important as the attending physician who signs the birth certificate. Do your part in the process, and leave the rest to God.

People aren't always where they appear to be. For instance, some who seem very religious are far from God in their hearts. Others, who act like "minus tens" are really "minus ones" on the faith continuum—under conviction. Never discount the possibility that God is doing something significant, even when it doesn't seem evident.

2/11/24

THE STRUGGLE TO FIND GOD

This long journey is not a matter of our struggle to find God, but rather to hide from him. Poet Francis Thompson described his flight from "The Hound of Heaven" this way: "I fled him, down the nights and down the days; / I fled him, down the arches of the years; / I fled him, down the labyrinthine ways / Of my own mind; and in the midst of tears."[3]

Sometimes, it takes awhile for truth to catch up.

FRED—A KEEPER

I was heading out the door for Ashland, Wisconsin, when the phone rang.

"My friend Fred needs a ride to detox," the caller explained. "There's a place reserved for him in Ashland. Do you know of anyone who could possibly take him?"

"You dialed the right number today! I'm going there now and will pick him up on the way. I'm happy for the company."

"Well, I must warn you, he may not be pleasant company. Fred's not too keen on religion."

"I won't be offended by anything he says."

Shortly after helping Fred into my car, I realized what the caller meant. Fred philosophized all the way to Ashland, sharing his opinions of preachers, churches, television evangelists, and fundamentalists. I just kept driving, smiling, and nodding.

"Uh huh."

By the end of the ride, he had warmed up to me. "You're a pretty good fellow for a preacher," Fred said, and even let me pray for him before entering the treatment center. This one-hour journey together, by divine appointment, birthed a beautiful friendship.

When Fred dried out, he began attending church. He raised good questions because he wanted to make sure Christ and common sense were compatible. Eventually, Fred embraced faith personally and became a member of our congregation.

One October, for pastor appreciation, Fred brought me a framed print of Ron Dicianni's *The Prodigal*. "That's me," he stated, pointing to the repentant son in his father's embrace. "Thank you for embracing me and helping me come home."

"And thank you for including me in your life," I replied. "I cherish our friendship."

Today, as I write this, Fred is housebound, with physical ailments, in the twilight of his years, but he keeps the faith. His precious wife, Donna, stays by his side, providing tender care, and they read the Bible and pray together daily.

A few years ago, Fred took me on a Lake Superior fishing excursion, along with my sons, Adam and Ryan. It was one of our greatest fish days ever. We landed some real beauties, including two huge lake trout, caught with one swoop of the net. Heading toward shore, in the setting sun, I lifted a prayer of thanks for my good friend, Fred—a keeper—who had been netted by love and brought into God's boat.

FISHERMAN'S PRAYER

"I pray that I may live to fish until my dying day.
And when it comes to my last cast, I then most humbly pray:
When in the Lord's great landing net and peacefully asleep
That in his mercy I be judged big enough to keep."[4]

16
BE a WITNESS, NOT the JUDGE

THE THINGS FISHERMEN KNOW ABOUT TROUT AREN'T
FACTS BUT ARTICLES OF FAITH.

—JOHN GIERACH

Some church folks, as Marshall Shelley observed, are "well-intentioned dragons."[1] Their earnest desire for setting things (and people) right comes off wrong. "Nothing has done greater damage to our Christian testimony," said Watchman Nee, "than our trying to be right and demanding right of others."[2]

A Barna Group survey conducted a few years ago found that 90 percent of non-Christian young people between the ages of sixteen and twenty-nine view Christians as judgmental.[3] Perhaps one reason for this is because we have assumed the wrong role in the courthouse. We play the part of judge, jury, or prosecuting attorney, rather than witness.

JUDGE

It's tempting to assume the role of judge, especially when so many evils abound. But if you find yourself pounding the gavel, you'd better step off the bench. Jesus warned us not to judge or we will be judged (Matt. 7:1). God alone is the judge—not us. That's quite a relief. Who in their right mind wants to carry such a burden of responsibility anyway? "There is no point trying to size people up," said Ann Voskamp, "because souls defy measuring."[4]

JURY

Some church people see themselves as self-selected juries, but it's not our job to convict people. That role belongs to the Holy Spirit. There is a huge difference between conviction by the Holy Spirit and condemnation by a narrow group of priggish people with shriveled hearts.

PROSECUTING ATTORNEY

Others take the prosecutor position: "You are guilty, and I'm going to prove it." Prosecutors are the ones who protest with placards and engage in heated arguments about religion. That approach is terribly ineffective. I have never seen a soul argued into God's kingdom. When you become the spiritual prosecutor, you are not assuming God's role at that point—but rather, the Devil's. He is "the accuser" (Rev. 12:10).

WITNESS

Your role as a Christ-follower is to simply be a witness. You don't have to pound gavels, point fingers, or cast blame. All you need to do is share your story. The beautiful thing about sharing your faith story is that nobody can deny it. No one can argue with your own personal experience. When you share personally, it touches hearts deeply. What is most personal is most universal.

We are not called to push anybody into our way of thinking. Rather, we bear witness to what God has done for us, and then leave the outcome in his hands.

"Evangelism is less about trying to manage an outcome as it is sharing events and offering an advent alternative for what everyone clearly sees," said Leonard Sweet. "Rather than wrestling the sinner's prayer out of a person who will say anything to get out of the headlock, it is a nudge toward the undeniable truth that is alive in all of us."[5]

Like the redeemed beggar, all you need to say is, "One thing I do know. I was blind but now I see!" (John 9:25).

These are a few pointers on sharing your faith story:

1. Pray that God will open doors for you to share.

2. When the door opens, have courage to speak.

3. Stay humble and never portray an attitude of superiority.

4. Keep it simple and brief. Don't share more than they want to know.

5. Tell them what you experienced, rather than what they should do.

6. Focus on the message (Jesus) rather than the mess.

7. Don't engage in argument. If they protest what you're saying, back off and let the Holy Spirit work.

17

YOU ARE

THE

SECOND WITNESS

WHAT COUNTS IN EVANGELISM IS NOT COGNITION,
BUT RECOGNITION. CAN WE IDENTIFY THE FACE
OF CHRIST WHEN HE SHOWS IT TO US?

—LEONARD SWEET

Your role, as noted in the last chapter, is to be a witness, rather than judge, jury, or prosecuting attorney. All you have to do is simply share what Jesus has done for you. No pressure.

And it gets even better than that! You don't have to take the stand as the primary witness. No, you are the second witness. The Holy Spirit bears witness first, and what you share is merely corroborating evidence.[1] The Spirit of God goes before us and opens doors. All we have to do is follow and put exclamation marks on what the Spirit is already doing and saying.

This liberating concept means when we follow the divine nudge, we'll never go cold turkey. God is already at work, preparing the way ahead of us. His prevenient grace tills the soil of human hearts to receive our message.

MIINAANZO-GIIGOONH

Miinaanzo-giigoonh means "purple fish" in the Ojibwe language and reminds me of Tiffiny, a direct descendent of Great Chief Buffalo.

I first met Tiffiny during a visit to our mentoring program for single moms. "I don't go to church, I don't believe in Jesus, and I don't like Christians very much," she said. "But I like you people. You make me feel safe."

Tiffiny's new friends loved and accepted her unconditionally. Over time, through several significant conversations, she began to consider Christ.

One morning, while preparing for work, a surprising thought came, uninvited, into her mind. "This would be a good day to give your life to Jesus."

"No, that's not for me. I was raised in the traditional Native way."

"This would be a good day to give your life to Jesus."

"I can't do something crazy like that."

"This would be a good day to give your life to Jesus."

"No, I won't do it unless I get a definite sign."

Driving to work, Tiffiny looked up and gasped. A bald eagle, the Creator's majestic messenger, circled in the sky.

"This would be a good day to give your life to Jesus."

Instead of going to work, Tiffiny drove directly to the church and found Pastor Loretta in her office.

"This would be a good day for me to give my life to Jesus," Tiffiny said.

And she did.

Loretta was the second witness, confirming what God had already spoken so powerfully in Tiffiny's heart.

"HELP HIM CATCH A FISH"

One summer Saturday, Steve, a fairly irreligious guy, took his nephew, Ethan, out in a boat, to catch his first fish. Unfortunately, they didn't get a nibble.

As the day drew to an end, Steve whispered a prayer. "God, if you are up there, please help Ethan catch a fish, and I promise to go to church tomorrow."

Before he said amen, the boy's bobber went under. Ethan had a bluegill on the line!

True to his promise, Steve attended Hayward Wesleyan Church the next day and eventually joined a small group. A deep thinker,

Steve had several soul-searching questions concerning God, faith, and the Bible. Fortunately, God matched him with Rob, an insightful small group leader who answered Steve's questions intelligently and guided him gently in the truth.

Rob, the second witness, simply confirmed what God was already saying to Steve.

THE NUDGE AT LINDON LANDING

On Round Lake one July night, as my fishing guide friend, Jim, approached Lindon Landing, he saw a solitary woman standing on the dock, gazing at the stars. She appeared troubled.

Jim, being a quiet and soft-spoken man, normally minds his own business and wouldn't think of bothering a stranger. But an inner nudge prompted him to engage in conversation.

"I noticed you standing there, and you seem heavyhearted. Is there something wrong?"

"Today, the doctor told me I have incurable cancer, and I don't know what to do," replied Donna.

"Do you have a support system of friends?"

"Not really—just my son and me."

"Well, it's no coincidence we met here this evening. God can help you through this. My wife, Tammy, is a parish nurse, and our friend Lori recently started a cancer support group. Could I introduce you to them?"

Donna agreed, "I would like that."

So Jim took her number, promising his wife would call soon.

The client in Jim's boat, observing this interaction, marveled, "That was a very good thing you just did."

The good thing continued. Tammy called and then met with Donna. Eventually, she helped her connect with Lori and the support group, whose members enfolded her without hesitation. Together, they provided compassionate care and invaluable assistance over the next several months. Tammy, Lori, and others called, visited, and filled the gaps wherever they could. As Donna's health deteriorated, they rallied around her and increased their support.

Late one night, Donna's teenage son called from Hayward Hospital.

"Mom's dying. The nurse said it will be any minute."

"I'll come right over. Are you alone with her?"

"No, we're not alone. Mom's best friends are here."

When I entered the room, I found Tammy and Lori keeping vigil.

Because Jim followed a nudge at Lindon Landing, Donna died in peace, surrounded by caring friends.

God goes first and opens the way. He loves us too much to let us go.

CAUGHT ON GOD'S HOOK

Along this line, I appreciate the following thought from German theologian, Meister Eckhart:

God lies in wait for us with nothing so much as with love. For love resembles the fisherman's hook. The fisherman cannot get the fish till it is caught on the hook. Once it takes the hook, he is sure of the fish; twist and turn as it may, this way or that, he is assured of his catch. And so I say of love: he who is caught by it has the strongest of bonds, and yet a pleasant burden. He who has taken up this sweet burden fares further and makes more progress than by all the harsh practices any men use. And, too, he can cheerfully bear and endure all that befalls him, whatever God inflicts on him, and can also cheerfully forgive whatever evil is done to him. Nothing brings you closer to God or makes God so much your own as the sweet bond of love. A man who has found this way need seek no other. He who hangs on this hook is caught so fast that foot and hand, mouth, eyes and heart, and all that is man's, belongs only to God.[2]

THE BEST FISHING GUIDE

Fishing goes better with a good guide. We have the best fishing guide available in the Holy Spirit. Jesus said, "When he, the

Spirit of truth, comes, he will guide you into all truth" (John 16:13 NIV84). We can trust him to guide us to the right people and places. He also directs us in how to share the gospel with sensitivity, courage, wisdom, and discernment. Beautiful things happen when we cooperate with God in his holy mission.

Here's a great prayer to start the day: "Jesus, what are you up to today? Can I join you?" You'll be surprised at the divine appointments you will encounter.

18
BE YOU
AND
LET THEM BE THEM

THERE ARE MANY GOOD FISHERMEN AND SOME GREAT
ONES. BUT THERE IS ONLY ONE YOU.

—ERNEST HEMINGWAY

No two humans are exactly alike; we're all unique. When sharing
Christ, be yourself and respect others for who they are.

BE YOU

Be who you are and don't try to be somebody else. When it
comes to sharing Christ's love, it's best to use an approach that

fits your unique temperament and personality. God wants to use you, with your perspective and style, to bring his love to people like you. Despite what many believe, extroverted, type A sales-types don't have a corner on the gospel market.

God has a special mission for noisy evangelists. He has a mission for quiet ones too. God uses introverts and extroverts in different ways. Find your own voice, and grant grace to yourself as well as to others in this regard.

IT TAKES ALL TYPES

My buddy Jim bubbles over with Jesus, and scatters gospel tracts everywhere, like Johnny Appleseed. I found one of Jim's pamphlets in a bathroom stall two hours from home. In the john, like John the Baptist, he had gone ahead, preparing the way of the Lord. Jim also has Christian slogans plastered on his pickup and a front-yard billboard advertising: "Jesus Is the Way to Heaven: Road Maps Available Here."

Jim's style is not mine. He has his own unique way of doing things. Jim came to Christ because a friend shared a gospel tract years ago, so he's simply returning the favor. He's a bit loud in his faith—but it's a happy loudness—and I know of at least a half dozen young men who found Jesus in jail and a couple of Zambian villages with fresh drinking water because Jim cared enough to step in and make a difference.

It is said that someone once grumbled to D. L. Moody, "I don't like your method of evangelism."

"What's yours?" Moody responded.

"I don't have any."

Moody replied, "Then I like my mine better than yours."

LET THEM BE THEM

It's also important to understand that each person we meet is a unique, one-of-a-kind individual. When bringing God's love, we should meet them where they are and give them what they need.

Jesus, our perfect example, varied his approach depending on the person. He didn't memorize a script. Jesus connected with Zacchaeus one way and a very different way with Nicodemus. His approach with the woman at the well was different than the rich young ruler. Salvation is personal, so Jesus made a very personal approach, tailor-made for each situation.

Failure in discerning what the other person needs leads to misunderstanding all the way around. When we are unaware, our attempts to help are unhelpful, and our intentions to bless feel more like a curse.

This is why my Ojibwe friends say, "Beware of the white man coming toward you with a gleam in his eye, wanting to help. Run as fast as you can in the opposite direction!"

THE MONKEY AND THE FISH

Dave Gibbons shared a great example of such unhelpful helpfulness in an Eastern parable, *The Monkey and the Fish*:

A typhoon stranded a monkey on an island. In a protected place on the shore, while waiting for the raging waters to recede, he spotted a fish swimming against the current. It seemed to the monkey that the fish was struggling and needed assistance. Being of kind heart, the monkey resolved to help the fish. A tree leaned precariously over the spot where the fish seemed to be struggling. At considerable risk to himself, the monkey moved far out on a limb, reached down, and snatched the fish from the waters. Scurrying back to the safety of his shelter, he carefully laid the fish on dry ground. For a few moments, the fish showed excitement but soon settled into a peaceful rest.[1]

Evangelism is not about turning people into someone else. Instead, it is helping them become the best versions of who they really are.

19

PEOPLE ARE NOT PROJECTS

CAUTION IS A MOST VALUABLE ASSET IN FISHING,
ESPECIALLY IF YOU ARE THE FISH.

—ANONYMOUS

Two determined women with *Watchtower* magazines showed up on our doorstep one Saturday afternoon. "Hello, we are in your neighborhood discussing the Bible . . . and with all the horrible things going on the world right now—"

"I'm sorry, but we're not interested," I interrupted and quickly shut the door. They shook the dust from their feet and moved on to Ray's place, across the street.

A half hour later, there was another knock. This time, I was met with two friends from church bearing cookies.

"Come in!" I greeted them warmly, "I'm so glad you came."

Later, I pondered the events of the day. Why did I shut the door on the first pair and welcome the second? Here's the primary difference: To my first visitors, I was a project; and to the second pair, I was a friend. (Also, I might add, the cookies helped. Door-to-door evangelists would get a much warmer reception if they brought dessert.)

NOBODY WANTS TO BE A PROJECT

Here's the bottom line: Nobody wants to be a project. Have you ever been someone's project? Felt crummy, didn't it? Why would we think others would feel any better about being our project?

Each individual is valuable and deserves respect. This means treating everybody with dignity. Nobody is drawn to Jesus by being disregarded or judged. As Jonathan Buckland observed, "How you say what you say will determine who will listen to what you say."[1]

When we objectify people, we discount their value.

ARTS OF SPIRITUAL CONVERSATION

I appreciate what Mary Schaller and the folks at Q Place are doing to help Christians connect with nonbelievers in a genuine and respectful manner, by simply following the practices of Jesus:

1. Jesus noticed people.
2. He prayed for them.
3. He listened.
4. He asked questions.
5. He loved them.
6. He welcomed them.
7. He facilitated good conversations.
8. He served with people who were willing to spend time with him.
9. He shared the good news about the kingdom of God.[2]

In other words, it starts with understanding rather than telling. "When genuine love is released in a relationship, God's presence is manifest," said Peter Scazerro. "The separate space between us becomes sacred space."[3]

Be intentional...

FOLLOW HIDDEN PATHS, FISH DEEP WEEDS

PURSUE SOME PATH, HOWEVER NARROW AND CROOKED,
IN WHICH YOU CAN WALK WITH LOVE AND REVERENCE.

—HENRY DAVID THOREAU

My daughter, Hannah, and I attended Cabela's 2013 North American Bass Circuit Championship on the Chippewa Flowage and cheered for the professionals as they presented their haul. The lucky guys who netted a fourteen-thousand-dollar grand prize with their boatload of lunkers said, "We found them by fishing deep weeds."

You will find lost, broken, and hurting people in deep weeds too. We're more inclined to look up when things are looking down.

DEEP WEEDS

In what kinds of weeds will we find God's purple fish?

Suffering

Pain opens the spirit. I've prayed with hundreds of people in the hospital over the years. Only one patient turned me down. Hospitals have chaplains for a good reason. Painful experiences open the soul's windows.

Sorrow

In times of loss, people need spiritual solace. The Spirit of God is our comforter as we walk the valley of grief. Deep ministry happens in the depths of sorrow. Some of my most profound ministry moments occurred at the funeral parlor. "Blessed are those who mourn, for they will be comforted" (Matt. 5:4).

Transition

During seasons of change, such as divorce, moving, the empty nest, or unemployment, people are especially open to spiritual matters. Even positive changes like marriage and childbirth bring stress, making us more tenderhearted and open. In transition times, people need clarity and direction. Christ stands as the solid rock for those overwhelmed by uncertainties.

Loneliness

One of the beautiful things about the Christian faith is that a family comes with it. "God sets the lonely in families" (Ps. 68:6). When my friend Charlie joined the church, he beamed, "I have a huge family now!"

HIDDEN PATHS

Besides a fleet of weather-beaten canoes, our family doesn't own a boat, but we find our way to the fish. We've discovered a few secret spots, which usually require a hike. When showing pictures of fish from these excursions, we're often asked, "Where did you catch them?" Our standard answer is, "Lake Wish-u-knew." Many of the best fishing holes are far from the highway, through bramble and brush, but if you look closely, you'll find a hidden path. Follow the path, and find the fish. A good fishing hole is worth the hike.

The path to deep weeds (suffering, sorrow, transition, and loneliness) is obvious. Pain, which C. S. Lewis called God's "megaphone," clearly marks a trail to God.[1] We are hardwired to seek spiritual relief from stress and pressure. But what about the people who are doing well? How do we bring God's love to those who don't seem to need anything? For those friends clipping right along without any sense of spiritual need, it's best to seek the hidden paths of beautiful inspiration.

Encouragement

Remember that everyone you meet carries a burden of some sort and needs encouragement. Those who appear to have it all together may be falling apart on the inside. Sooner or later, we all face adversity, disappointment, and heartache.

3|17|24

Sacrifice

Everyone, even the sour cynic, is touched deeply when they observe someone willing to give themselves for others. Sacrifice is beautiful and inspiring. This is why there's a catch in our throats when veterans and rescue workers are honored. It's the reason people like Mother Teresa and Martin Luther King, Jr. are recognized. They stand as role models of selflessness, reminding us that's how we're supposed to be.

Service

We all want to be wanted and need to be needed. Most people respond positively when invited to participate in acts of kindness for others. I know several people who embraced faith while on missions of mercy. Helping those in need is very Jesus-like. You can't serve others without being changed in the process.

Art

Artistic expression is close to God's heart. In fact, the first verb in the Bible is *created* (Gen. 1:1). This is why music, poetry, and dance move the soul so deeply. It was art, rather than argument, that captured the heart of Peter Hitchens. Peter shared the atheism of his famous brother, Christopher, until, encountering Rogier van der Weyden's fifteenth-century painting *Last Judgment*, he experienced a spiritual awakening. It was more horrifying than beautiful, but impressed spiritual realities upon him.[2]

Nature

The beauty of rivers, lakes, and wildlife inspires all who visit. When I need to have my soul stirred, I walk in the forest, which displays God's grandeur better than any cathedral. "Wilderness," said Sigurd Olson, the great Northwoods naturalist, "is a spiritual necessity . . . a means of regaining serenity and equilibrium."[3]

SUNSET AT FISH CREEK

While vacationing in Door County, Cathy and I went on a "fish boil" date in a quaint village called Fish Creek. "Fish boil" doesn't sound too romantic, but it was memorable nonetheless — and better than it sounds.

Holding hands on our way back to the car, I noticed a little trail leading into the woods with a sign pointing to Sunset Beach. Curiosity got the best of us, so we followed the hidden path through a maze of jack pines and ended up at a small park overlooking Green Bay.

The sun, slowly sinking in the west, created breathtaking blends of orange, purple, red, and black. A masterpiece of art was being painted before our eyes.

About seventy-five people gathered at Sunset Beach that evening, observing the majesty in hushed reverence. We were total strangers, yet somehow felt like family, or perhaps a congregation.

"This is like church," Cathy whispered, and I nodded. It felt similar to when we entered Westminster Abbey a few months prior. Yes, like a cathedral, only better.

"I should take an offering," I whispered back and received an elbow in the ribs.

A loon glided silently before us, her haunting call echoing across the lake. The orange sun took a final bow and settled below the horizon. Spontaneously, the crowd broke into applause and ambled away.

I said, "Amen."

Cathy and I lingered awhile, her head nestled gently on my shoulder. At that tender moment, I loved her more than ever, recalling the words of C. S. Lewis: "Music and poetry—the mere face of a girl, the song of a bird, or the sight of a horizon—are always blowing [evil's] whole structure away."[4]

21
RESPECT BOUNDARIES

YOU WILL FIND ANGLING TO BE LIKE THE VIRTUE OF
HUMILITY,
WHICH HAS A CALMNESS OF SPIRIT AND A WORLD OF
OTHER BLESSINGS ATTENDING UPON IT.

—IZAAK WALTON

"People AREN'T going to remember what you say, BUT THEY WILL Remember How you made Them feel."

I served as a kids' camp counselor for a few years. From time to time, events unfolded that were downright traumatic. One night, for instance, a wolf spider escaped its box cage and terrorized the entire cabin. Another time, capture the flag sent three kids to the emergency room. Once, a triple-dog-dare led to an ant eating contest.

UNCLE HARVEY'S ALTAR CALL

However, the most traumatic camp experience we ever had was Uncle Harvey's altar call. After a heart-wrenching story, Uncle Harvey, sweating profusely, put the pressure on: "Unless you kids come up to accept Jeeeezus tonight, you're going to die in your sins and go straight to hell! If you don't want to burn forever in the lake of fire, get up here right now, kneel down, and confess your sins before almighty God. Maybe he will have mercy on you."

Dozens of vile prepubescent sinners came to the altar, sobbing and repenting, while Uncle Harvey rejoiced over being responsible for such a great harvest of souls.

Although I'm totally in favor of extending invitations to Jesus, something just seemed wrong about Harvey's approach. God uses all types, and I'm sure Uncle Harvey meant well, but he missed a few cues. Scaring the bejeebers out of kids isn't the most effective method of child evangelism.

Like several other evangelists I've encountered, Uncle Harvey, unaware of social boundaries, was completely oblivious when he overstepped them.

LAYERS OF PERMISSION GIVING

All of us have several layers of hospitality defined by social boundaries. For instance, if some guy on the street acts crazy, you probably don't want him on your property. You're likely to leave door-to-door vacuum salesmen outside on the step. You may keep an acquaintance in your entryway, share your table with a friend, and give family members refrigerator rights. Someone who crosses boundaries without permission is trespassing. Stepping into space where hospitality is not extended is rude and intrusive.

When it comes to faith sharing, there are several layers of permission giving, and you should not trespass beyond the area you have been invited to enter. Knock gently and then follow the hints from the other person concerning how deep the conversation goes.

According to Dr. Gary Chapman, there are five levels of communication:

- Level 1: Hallway Talk—"Fine, how are you?"
- Level 2: Reporter Talk—"Just give me the facts."
- Level 3: Intellectual Talk—"Do you know what I think?"
- Level 4: Emotional Talk—"Let me tell you how I feel."
- Level 5: Loving, Genuine Truth Talk—"Let's be honest."[1]

Depth of conversation is based entirely on the level of trust. Nobody wants to share deeply with someone they don't trust. This is perhaps the biggest problem with the popular evangelism pick-up line, "If you died tonight, do you know whether or not you'll go to heaven?" That's trespassing by four levels and often leads to resentment rather than conversion.

Occasionally, I've experienced conversations that immediately went from level 1 to level 5, but normally, deeper communication comes over a stretch of time as trust develops.

It's common for people to not go beyond level 2 or 3 with *anybody*—even their spouse and kids—so there's no way they're going to open up deeply with a total stranger or mere acquaintance. What does this mean for us when it comes to sharing the gospel?

1. Have courage to gently knock at the gate of the next level, but if they don't open it, just meet them where they are willing to meet you.

2. You are more likely to have level 5 spiritual conversations with those who feel close and safe with you.

3. As trust is established, the conversation deepens. Usually it takes a long time, but sometimes it can happen very quickly. If they start opening up, don't shrink back from taking it to a deeper level.

4. Follow R. A. Torrey's advice: First, obey the Holy Spirit. If you have a nudge to share Jesus, it is more likely the Holy Spirit than the flesh or the Devil. Second, never embarrass the other person.[2] In other words, follow the Golden Rule. Treat others the way you wish to be treated, with the same kindness you show your friends.

Along this line, I appreciate Miroslav Volf's insights concerning interfaith dialogue: "The bonds of affection in friendship will shape one's way of witnessing—make it respectful, considerate, and loving. The value of the friendship militates against any sort of witnessing that will be deeply disrespectful and harmful of the other. We would suggest that Christians ought to take how they would witness to a friend to be paradigmatic of how they should witness in general."[3]

22
SEEK
COMMON GROUND

I PREFER TO MEET FISH WHERE THEY ARE, AS THEY ARE.

—CASCADE KID

Treat everyone with respect, and meet people where they are. This encounter counts, so don't blow it with self-righteous judgmentalism or an air of superiority. "Like it or not," said Christian Piatt, "you represent the entirety of Christianity to that person in that moment; that's a lot of responsibility."[1]

START WITH HURTING

God's purple fish—those he treasures most—are lost, broken, and hurting people. That includes everybody you meet. When we engage in spiritual conversation with lost, broken, hurting people, it's best to start with hurting.

If you start with lost, then your job is to set them straight. That means you know something and they don't. In other words, you assume you're smart and they're stupid.

If you start with broken, then your job is to fix them. The unspoken message is that broken things are problems, less valuable, and may be beyond repair.

But when you start with hurting, your job is to bring healing.

People resent those who try to fix them or make them feel stupid but respect those who bring a healing presence. That's what Jesus did. He started with healing, and then moved from there to straighten and repair. The healing came first.

There is a direct connection between spirituality and healing. Airdre Grant, in the *Journal of the Australian Traditional Medicine Society*, wrote, "Spirituality and religion belong in the healing paradigm; they are determinants of health and they are factors in recovery, well-being, and longevity."[2] When we begin with healing, we follow the Jesus path and find a strong connection.

Distressed people will avoid you if they perceive you are trying to change or correct them. If, on the other hand, through kind words, gentle touch, and understanding, you bring healing and grace to their painful situations, they will seek you out.

In order to find common ground with someone who does not claim Christ, the best thing to do is leave your agenda behind. Build relationships with nonbelievers for the sake of the relationship, without any personal agenda except encouragement, love, and blessings.

EMBRACE OUR COMMON HUMANITY

Look for what you have in common, rather than focusing on your differences. "If we focus on Jesus as the center, then the key question becomes whether someone is oriented toward him or away from him," said John Ortberg. "We realize that God is in a much better position than we are to know who's in and who's out. We also realize that everyone has something to learn, that everyone has a next step to take, and we don't have to make ourselves seem more different than we really are. We embrace our common humanity."[3]

This hit home with me several months ago when I was called to help and comfort a distressed young man. We had plenty of differences, but reflecting on the experience later, through the lens of Christ's love, I wrote the following poem:

He is young—I am middle-aged.
He is agnostic—I am a Christian.

He is gay—I hold to traditional marriage.

He is hurting—I care.

He needs grace—I need grace.

He is a human being—I am a human being.

Sacred love covers the difference.

FIND THE CONNECTING POINT

Everybody has a story. There is always a connection, if you are willing to be humble, respectful, and genuinely interested. Sometimes, when it feels like you're from two different planets, you have to work hard to find the connecting point.

The acrostic FISH suggests areas where we might find common ground:

- F—Family
- I—Interests
- S—Situations
- H—Hurts

See if you can discover something about their family, interests, situations, and hurts, without being intrusive. There's a good chance you share similar experiences and will find bridges of understanding there.

BAREFOOT WEDDING

One July Saturday, I conducted an outdoor wedding on the shore of Beaver Lake. It was a pretty rough crowd, and they didn't seem too spiritually minded. Just before the ceremony, the bride spoke up, motioning to the wedding party, "This is a barefoot wedding, so I want you guys to remove your shoes."

"How about me?" I wondered. "Can I join you?"

"Oh, no, Pastor," she replied. "I didn't mean you had to take off *your* shoes."

"But would it be OK if I was barefoot with you?"

"Really? You would do that for me?"

"Of course," I said. "Sounds fun."

"I never imagined a man of the cloth would take off his shoes for a wedding."

"And I have never done it that way before, but there's a first time for everything."

So I slipped off my shoes and performed the wedding in a suit and bare feet. I felt silly, especially when they snapped pictures, but was glad to be a part of it with them. In fact, my shoe removal brought immediate acceptance into their inner circle. Then it dawned on me. This was holy ground, like Moses experienced when he took off his shoes.

After signing the marriage license, I put my loafers back on and headed toward the car. Two groomsmen stood near a tree guzzling beer. As I passed, one shouted, "Hey, Preacher, I think it was pretty cool what you did." Then, lowering his voice he continued, "When you say your prayers tonight, would you remember me?"

"I sure will."

He nodded, gulped back a tear, smiled big, and raised his Budweiser toward me in salute.

I smiled, nodded, and raised my Bible in return.

23

THINK LIKE

A

FISH

I'M PRETTY GOOD WITH A ROD, BUT I NEED THREE MORE
YEARS BEFORE I CAN THINK LIKE A FISH.

—NORMAN MACLEAN

As far as I'm concerned, my buddy Cody Conner is among the greatest fishermen on the planet. The best day fishing I ever had was with Cody on the Namekagon, when he took me downriver in a canoe and pointed where to cast.

The fishing trip was my payment for officiating his wedding. During the ceremony, I blackmailed him. "I have two wedding sermons, Cody, and it is entirely up to you which one I use. Since you love fishing so much, I have a long wedding sermon with a point for each letter in the word *muskellunge*. I also have much shorter version using the word *musky*. If you promise to take me fishing, I'll give the short one."

That was a no-brainer for Cody. He accepted my larceny, and thus we found ourselves floating down the river, hauling in bass and walleyes left and right. For me, it was fishing heaven. For Cody, it was just a normal day on the river. He catches fish like that all the time.

Reflecting on what makes Cody different from most anglers, I concluded that it's the way he thinks. Cody doesn't think like a fisherman; he thinks like a fish. Instead of focusing on himself and his own personal comfort, he continually asks, "Where are the fish right now? What are they feeling? When will they be most likely to bite? Under the present conditions, what bait will be most attractive to them?"

Cody finds fish because he thinks like them and then goes searching for them. He doesn't allow small hindrances that deter lesser anglers, such as inconvenient timing or inclement weather, to get in the way. If it's good for the fish, it's good for Cody.

QUIT FISHING IN THE BATHTUB

To find fish, you must think like them and make the extra effort to go get them. There are no fish in your bathtub, so you might as well not fish there. You won't catch anything but rubber ducks and soap bubbles. You have to get out of the house to find the fish. I've never had a fish knock at my door, asking to come in. If I want to find fish, I need to go get them.

The first two letters in the word *gospel* spell *go*. I can't expect them to come to me. Too many Christians are content with staying at home, waiting for the fish to show up. The isolated evangelical bubble keeps us from meaningful relationship with those who do not share our faith perspective.

Entire congregations become ingrown, with resources and programming energy going to perpetuate the status quo. Then they scratch their heads and wonder why so few seem interested. Instead of being fishers of people, we've become keepers of the aquarium.[1] The primary reason so many churches have not reached anyone new is because so few reach out beyond themselves.

If you are a pastor, you must lead the way in this. Don't spend all your time in the office. The view of the world is extremely limited from behind a desk. You need a much broader perspective than that. Start thinking like a fish. Get out of the house and go find some people. Your office will run just fine in your absence and will still be there when you return.

IN A BARREL AND UP A TREE

The nineteenth-century evangelist "Uncle John" Vassar thought like a fish and spent a good portion of his ministry out of the house. One day, he went to a neighbor's farm to speak with him about the condition of his soul. The wayward farmer saw him coming, escaped out the back door, ran to a shed, and hid in a hogshead, a barrel. Undeterred, Uncle John chased the man, climbed into the barrel with him, held a prayer meeting, and led the man to Jesus. I suppose you could say that was like shooting purple fish in a barrel.

That's the approach Jesus took when he went to Jericho searching for a lost treasure: Zacchaeus, the vertically challenged tax collector. Thinking like the little guy, Jesus went after Zacchaeus and found him up a tree (Luke 19:1–9). After this search and rescue, Jesus summed it up by saying, "The Son of Man came to seek and to save the lost" (v. 10).

Think like a fish, and then go get them.

24

USE WORDS
WHEN NECESSARY

PREACH THE GOSPEL AT ALL TIMES,
AND WHEN NECESSARY, USE WORDS.

—ST. FRANCIS OF ASSISI

A worried mother, dropping her daughter off for her freshman year at the university, said, "I'm concerned they will make fun of you for being a Christian."

Her daughter replied, "Don't worry, Mom, no one will ever know."

Silence, when it comes to undercover Christianity, isn't always golden. Sometimes, it's just plain yellow. Too many cowardly Christians hide behind the skirts of St. Francis.[1]

SPEAK WITH YOUR LIFE FIRST

Please don't misunderstand. Like St. Francis, I believe our lives should preach. Seeing a sermon is better than hearing one.

Someone expressed disappointment after attending the funeral of a well-known community member: "The pastor blew it. He had a great opportunity to share the gospel, and never got around to it."

I responded, "I guess you better not depend on the funeral preacher to give the gospel for you." It's better to live close to God, so your whole life preaches.

NOT CAREFUL BUT REAL

"I came to Christ by watching my neighbor," Ron said.

"Did he realize you were observing him?" I asked.

"No, but when I saw how he handled life, I wanted to be like him."

"Wow," I replied. "We need to be really careful how we live."

"Actually, he wasn't careful," Ron said. "He was just real."

If we're real, it just flows. If we're phony, then we have to be careful to put on a good Christian façade. Ron's friend was one of those described by the prophet Zechariah: "They will sparkle in his land like jewels in a crown. How attractive and beautiful they will be!" (Zech. 9:16–17).

NEXT DOOR TO THE REVEREND

Some time ago, I was called to the bedside of a dying woman in hospice care. She shared with me about life, family, and religion. Then she mentioned the pastor who lived next door. "I've lived next to the reverend for nearly ten years, and I've got to tell you—I'm not too impressed. He never greets me or even acknowledges my existence when we pass. The only time he ever speaks to me is when he is complaining about something. We've not had one positive, neighborly conversation. As far as I'm concerned, if a man's religion can't help him be a decent neighbor, then it ain't worth diddly squat."

I didn't know how to respond. I'm sure there's another side to the story, but my heart was heavy for the bitter, suffering woman. I also felt sad for the pastor, who, while diligently shepherding his congregation, had neglected the mission field at his very own doorstep.

Is the gospel you profess good news to your next-door neighbor?

SPEAK WITH YOUR WORDS

We need to live it out and speak it out. Let me rephrase St. Francis: "It's necessary—use words." If you only preach with your life and not your words, then those around you will think you're a nice person without understanding why.

Eventually, you must say something, if you're going to preach the gospel. Bible scholar Scot McKnight observed, "The words for evangelism in the New Testament, particularly when one focuses on the key 'gospeling' texts, are verbal proclamation words and not behavior words. I know of no text that says someone evangelized without saying a word, or that tells us someone announced the good news in how they lived."[2]

WHY DON'T WE USE WORDS?

Perhaps the reason we don't use our words to share Christ's love is because we don't want to seem weird. However, we're willing to talk about everything else we love. Conversation with friends naturally flows to what's most important. You talk about what you cherish. If you never say anything about Christ, how will your friends know he means anything to you?

Atheist comedian Penn Jillette shared an instance when a Christian fan witnessed to him after a show. Jillette speaks fondly of this experience. With tender respect, the man approached Jillette and handed him a New Testament inscribed with a personal message. Although the encounter did not change his mind about God's existence, it led the comedian to some deep introspection and this profound conclusion: "How much do you have to hate somebody to believe everlasting life is possible and not tell them that?"[3]

25

COMPASSION
DOES SOMETHING

WHEN YOU BAIT THE HOOK WITH YOUR HEART,
THE FISH ALWAYS BITES.

—JOHN BURROUGHS

My first sermon was a fog of confused ramblings. It went better rehearsing in front of the bathroom mirror. There I was Billy Graham, but on the spot, behind the sacred desk, I shriveled into Pee-Wee Herman. To the congregation's relief, it lasted only seven torturous minutes.

Halfway through my downward spiral, a lady in the back shouted, "Help him, Jesus!" In retrospect, I think she was begging the good Lord to help me land the thing and relieve us all from the misery.

Jesus did far better in his first shot as a rookie preacher. Nobody shouted, "Help him, Elijah!" Before a hometown crowd, Jesus asked for a scroll and read the following passage from Isaiah: "The Spirit of the Lord is on me, because he has anointed me to proclaim good news to the poor. He has sent me to proclaim freedom for the prisoners and recovery of sight for the blind, to set the oppressed free, to proclaim the year of the Lord's favor" (Luke 4:18–19; see Isa. 61:1–2). Then he delivered the punch line: "*Today* this scripture is fulfilled in your hearing" (Luke 4:21, emphasis added).

Jesus' first message, like mine, probably lasted around seven minutes, but unlike mine, he captured the essence of his entire ministry. The gospel isn't just for sometime in the distant future. It is immediate good news for those who struggle.

Jesus cares for the lost, broken, and hurting, and calls us to do the same. Following Jesus always leads to compassion— today.

COMPASSION FEELS SOMETHING

Compassion feels something called empathy. Empathy is putting yourself in another's shoes. Your sorrow becomes my sorrow. Your burden is my burden too.

"Compassion and pity are very different. Whereas compassion reflects the yearning of the heart to merge and take on some of the suffering, pity is a controlled set of thoughts designed to assure separateness. Compassion is the spontaneous response of love; pity, the involuntary reflex of fear."[1]

One night, while visiting a parishioner in the emergency room, I heard bone-chilling shrieks coming from the unit next door.

"Somebody help me. I hurt so bad. Please, please, help me."

Feeling sorry for the poor fellow, I wondered if I should do something.

"Don't bother," his nurse said. "He had too much to drink and was walking in snowdrifts with sneakers. His toes are frostbitten, but he'll be alright."

The man continued to cry out, but I followed the nurse's advice and decided not to bother.

I learned later the guy signed himself out, hitched a ride somewhere, and fell in a snow bank. They found his frozen body the next morning.

His pathetic cries still echo in my mind. I wish I could do that one over. What if I had listened to my heart and stepped in to help this troubled soul? His life may not have ended so tragically. Sometimes, we need to follow the compassion path, even when others say, "Don't bother."

COMPASSION DOES SOMETHING

Not only does compassion mean empathy, it also means action. Several times in the Gospels, we see Jesus being "moved" with compassion. Whenever Jesus saw a distressing situation, he didn't sit around feeling bad. He did something.

My soul stirs when I hear of someone going the extra mile for others, because this is the very heart of the Jesus message. Compassion does something.

The American Birkebeiner, the largest cross-country ski race in North America, ends in Hayward, Wisconsin. Every February, ten thousand nordic enthusiasts ski over fifty kilometers through the woods to the finish line on snow-covered Main Street, where spectators ring them in with cowbells.

The Birkie, as locals call it, commemorates the rescue of little Norwegian prince Haakon Haakonson in 1206. In a winter storm, two brave Birkebeiners (meaning birch leggings) whisked the royal toddler from hostile enemies. They skied fifty-five kilometers through treacherous mountains and deep forests to safety. Because they took the risk, the little prince was spared, and Haakon later returned to the throne, leading Norway into its golden age.

When I ring my cowbell at the finish line on Main Street, it's not just for sport, but for sacrifice.

One of the best examples of sacrifice I know is Leonard Wheeler, nineteenth-century missionary to the Ojibwe. He lived on Madeline Island and took mission trips to the mainland. The tribe warmly embraced Leonard, his wife Harriet, and their children.

The Wheelers taught school, developed gardens, cared for the sick, and ministered to emotional and spiritual needs. The brave minister successfully fought the government's effort to relocate the tribe west of the Mississippi and was instrumental in helping the Ojibwe retain treaty rights.

In February 1859, Wheeler learned that a ring of unscrupulous businessmen planned to steal the LCO Reservation land from the Native Americans. In arctic temperatures and a howling winter storm, Wheeler trekked 250 miles to Sparta on snowshoes on behalf of his friends, his feet cut and bleeding from the straps. He then caught a train to Washington, met with the Bureau of Indian Affairs, and shut down the wicked scheme.

Leonard lost a lung from this grueling ordeal, but he saved the reservation. He struggled with health issues the rest of his life but considered it a fair trade. "Greater love has no one than this: to lay down one's life [or lung] for one's friends" (John 15:13).

26
ICHTHYOPHOBIA: FACE YOUR FEARS

CONFIDENCE IS GOING AFTER MOBY DICK IN A ROW-
BOAT
AND TAKING THE TARTAR SAUCE WITH YOU.

—ZIG ZIGLAR

One great obstacle to sharing the gospel with others is spiritual ichthyophobia: the fear of fish. We must face our fears with courage if we are going to be effective in introducing others to Jesus. Courage, after all, is not the absence of fear, but "fear that has said its prayers."[1]

It is helpful for those embarking on fishing ventures to hear the patron saint of the deaf, Francis de Sales:

Go courageously to do whatever you are called to do.

If you have any fears, say to your soul:

"The Lord will provide for us."

If your weakness troubles you, cast yourselves

on God, and trust in him.

The apostles were mostly unlearned fishermen,

but God gave them learning enough

for the work they had to do.

Trust in him, depend on his providence; fear nothing.[2]

A key to overcoming fear is to identify it. What makes you afraid? Why? Naming your ichthyophobia is half the battle.

IDENTIFY YOUR FEARS

Many believers are terrified to share their faith because of their own negative personal encounters with obnoxious Christians, and they definitely don't want to become "one of *them*."

A couple came to me inquiring about church membership. "We don't have to become 'those born agains' to be members of your church, do we?" I was taken aback for a moment. I believe in a born-again experience. Jesus clearly said, "Unless you are born again, you cannot see the Kingdom of God" (John 3:3 NLT).

Then I asked a game-changing question: "What do you mean by 'those born agains'?"

"People like Aunt Agnes."

"Tell me about Aunt Agnes."

"She's a mean-spirited religious nut—a nasty, judgmental hypocrite."

"Oh . . . well . . . if *that's* what you mean, then no—you don't have to be one of *those* born agains." I went on to explain the new birth with a description that looked much more like Jesus than Aunt Agnes.

Rejection is another fear believers have about spiritual conversations. If the person you're speaking to is not open spiritually, there is a good chance what you say will be rejected. Don't take that personally. It's not you that he or she is rejecting, but rather the message you are trying to deliver. If you are shut down, just keep on loving him or her. Remember, it usually takes 7.6 conversations.

My former student, Wes, was a drug dealer in his B.C. days. Once, in the middle of a deal, someone knocked on his door. Everyone panicked and started hiding evidence. Wes grabbed his .45, looked through the peephole, and saw his wife's pastor standing on the doorstep.

"Hello, Wes," the pastor said. "I thought I'd drop by for a little visit."

"Uh . . . I'm kind of busy right now," Wes shouted through the door, somewhat relieved that it was the pastor rather than the police.

Later, he recalled, "The pastor left that day, but he didn't leave me alone. He kept coming back, and I kept turning him down. Then, one day, I opened the door, and he led me to Jesus."

A third fear many believers have is failure. If you view your role as just being the second witness, then you realize the outcome is not your responsibility. The performance pressure is off. Craig Groeschel said, "You don't fail when you invite people to repent and follow Christ and no one responds. You fail when you don't invite people to repent and follow Christ."[3] If an irreligious person becomes a little more open because of a warm interaction with you, that's no failure.

I planted jalapeños in my garden and checked on them regularly. The first time I looked, there were no peppers—not even a bloom. Was that a failure? Of course not. It takes time for peppers to sprout.

If you share Jesus and don't receive a positive response, just consider the other person a holy jalapeño that hasn't bloomed yet. Give it time and try again.

BEAT YOUR FEARS

Instead of beating yourself up over your fears, you can turn the tables and beat them.

Trust in God

Psalm 23 says, "I will fear no evil, for you are with me." God's presence brings calmness and eliminates anxiety. "When fear comes knocking at your door, let faith go to answer it, and no one will be there."[4]

Practice Courage

Be courageous, even if it scares you to death. "Build dikes of courage," said Martin Luther King, Jr., "to hold back the flood of fear."[5]

Love Sincerely

"Perfect love drives out fear" (1 John 4:18). If you love others, you will not fear them. If you love life, it will not terrify you. If you love the gospel, then sharing it will be an adventure rather than torture.

Move Forward

We cannot allow small fears to discourage and deter us from our mission. Move ahead. Keep plugging away. Dare to take the risk.

Life is too short to remain handcuffed to anxious stomach-churning thoughts. Break the chains, be bold, and conquer your fears today!

27
DRAW IN
THE
NET

WHEN THE BOBBER GOES UNDER, SET THE HOOK!

—UNCLE WOODY

Originally, I was going to call this chapter "Set the Hook," but somehow that seems a tad violent. You can push the fishing analogy only so far. Evangelism is much more like net fishing.

GROUP FISHING

I appreciate Leonard Sweet's observation that net fishing in the New Testament was social rather than solitary: "An entire village would fish together and often two boats would work in tandem drag-netting fish in between them."[1]

One of the greatest joys in a church is when people work together to draw their friends and neighbors to Jesus. I've seen groups of committed believers working the boats together on countless occasions.

Years ago, when I was a youth pastor, we did a Bible study on evangelism. I challenged the students to think of the most unlovable person in their school—the one who seemed furthest from grace. Then I asked them to consider inviting that person to youth group the following week.

The next Wednesday night, a new kid showed up. When I introduced myself, he said, "It's funny. I didn't think I had any friends, but fifteen different people invited me to youth group tonight."

So often in ministry and other helping professions we have an image of one serving many. For instance, one doctor serves many patients. One clerk assists many customers. One pastor serving many parishioners. But in God's kingdom, it's the other way around: many serving the one.[2]

It takes a village to raise a Christian.

GENTLE FISHING

A person can be in the net and not even realize it. Net fishing is gentle. Gordon attended church for several years before claiming the faith as his own. He said things like "you Christians," but we all knew he was already in the net. He just hadn't come to the realization. God meets us right where we are and gently nudges us forward. We must be patient with those who are still in the spiritual birthing process.

SET THE HOOK

There are occasions, however, when we need to switch to the pole and set the hook when the bobber goes under. If the Holy Spirit leads your conversation to a point of decision, don't be afraid to ask the person to cross the line of faith. An open door is an invitation.

One morning I made an appointment with a purple fish named Bob. We had been friends for years, but he always pushed spiritual matters aside. Then Bob had a life-threatening illness that landed him in the hospital. Shortly after his release, I took Bob to Norske Nook for breakfast. After swapping fish tales and discussing the Packers and politics, we got around to his recent health scare.

"Bob, you are certainly fortunate to have pulled through surgery the way you did," I told him.

"Well, I guess it wasn't my time to go yet."

Bob's bobber went under.

"If it had been your time to go, would you have been ready?"

Bob choked on his pancakes. After regaining composure, he responded honestly, "No, I wouldn't have been ready."

This opened the door for a meaningful conversation. At the end of our time together, Bob had not yet made the commitment to follow Jesus, but he was definitely on the line. A few weeks later, our mutual friend, Pastor Ben, reeled him in.

28

WHEN FISH
AREN'T BITING

AN HOUR OR TWO BY THE SIDE OF A CHALK STREAM IS
ALWAYS
DELIGHTFUL, WHETHER YOU CATCH FISH OR NOT.
—SIR WILMOT PARKER HERRINGHAM

I've returned empty-handed from fishing on countless occasions. Despite their best efforts, there are times when anglers don't catch fish. For me, that's every fishing season opener, the first Saturday of May. It's an annual ritual. I depart eagerly with high hopes and return home with nothing but the sniffles.

"Any bites?" Cathy asks.

"Lots," I reply, "from mosquitoes and horseflies."

I've had the same experience when sharing Jesus with others.

If you've tried to engage people in spiritual conversation but failed to help them experience the wonders of Christ's love, you're not alone. It's tempting to quit when it seems like you're getting nowhere.

What should we do if we see no results in our witnessing attempts? Louis Spray, who reputedly netted three record muskies in his day, had good advice for handling slow fishing times.[1]

KEEP CASTING

"If you've got the bait in the water," said Spray, "your percentage is better than if you're sittin' over on a log someplace smoking a cigarette."[2] In other words, don't give up and keep on fishing! Down through the years after taking worms for a swim without a nibble, I've often been ready to pack it up. Inevitably, one of my fishing buddies would say, "Just one last cast, Dad." Often that one last cast led to several more casts and a bucketful of fish.

When you share Christ's love with others without immediate results, don't get discouraged. Give it another cast.

CHANGE IT UP

If your approach isn't working, change it.

Jesus told his weary disciples, skunked after pulling an angling all-nighter, to cast their nets on the other side of the boat. They followed his advice, changed it up, and landed 153 keepers (see John 21).

"If you're casting a bait all day long, and you don't get nothin', you may get kind of sour at everybody and the world and yourself," Louis Spray said. "So change baits often and it will stir up the enthusiasm and will keep you from going to shore and making coffee."[3]

If spiritual fishing is slow, you may need to rethink your approach. Why don't they seem interested? Imagine what might work and try again.

When the great bassmaster, Al Lindner, came to speak at our church, the sanctuary was packed with irreligious anglers. They had come to hear about fish, and Al was fishing for them. That evening, Al made a bold statement. "I never get skunked," he said. "Every time I go fishing, I catch fish."

Now that was hard for the rest of us to imagine.

"Every single time?"

"Yes, every time."

Al continued, "You may believe 'the fish aren't biting today,' but I say the fish are *always* biting."

Now, he had our full attention.

"Yes, they are always biting. They just don't happen to be biting what you're offering them. If the fish aren't biting for you, change it up. The secret is in the presentation."

Al gave a splendid presentation that night, and several men opened their lives to Jesus. I'd say, the purple fish were biting.

FOLLOW THE NUDGE

When is the best time to go? Here's Louis Spray's experience: "As far as when the best time to go fishing is, I've caught big muskies during all times of the year—so I don't know what to say. My experience is that when you get the urge to go musky fishing, go out and you're liable to catch one."[4]

In other words, follow the nudge.

Leonard Sweet says, "I define evangelism as 'nudge' and evangelists as 'nudgers.' Evangelism is awakening each other to the God who is already there. Evangelism is nudging people to pay attention to the mission of God in their lives and to the necessity of responding to that initiative in ways that birth new realities."[5]

FISH IT CLEAN

Don't pack it up too soon. Persistence pays off. As Spray advised, "You've got to fish it clean."[6]

Some of the best spiritual conversations I've ever had were when I thought the conversation was over. Don't shut it down too quickly. They may be more open than you think.

Paraphrasing Ecclesiastes 11:1: "Keep casting your worms "BREAD" on the water."

RHYTHMS OF INTENTION

When you give it your best without positive results, it is easy to become discouraged, and feel your efforts were in vain. Do what you can, then leave the rest to God, remembering T. S. Eliot's line, "For us, there is only the trying. The rest is not our business."[7]

I find great comfort in Michael Cooper-White's encouragement for spiritually "slow fishing" times:

Some folks get disillusioned and disappointed if they fish and expect a big tug on the line every time the hook goes in the water. Some days there are only nibbles. Some days the line remains utterly still. If "success" is measured in some volume of "hits" or spiritual cargo carried home, the very quest for a catch will soon take on a driven nature and be counterproductive. But if one simply lives within the "Rhythms of Intention," sooner or later there likely will be some stirrings beneath the surface. And you will know that God is active in the world and concerned about your life. You will also recognize that it's not a matter of our "hooking God," but allowing ourselves to be more solidly netted by the Divine."[8]

FISHING TRIPS
AND
TREASURE HUNTS

FISHING IS NOT AN ESCAPE FROM LIFE,
BUT OFTEN A DEEPER IMMERSION INTO IT.

—HARRY MIDDLETON

"COME, FOLLOW ME," JESUS SAID,
"AND I WILL SEND YOU OUT TO FISH FOR PEOPLE."

—MATTHEW 4:19

29

TRACKING GOD'S WAYS

RIVER TIME IS SACRED SPACE.

—MICHAEL ATTAS

Jesus is already present in the lives of everyone around us. Our task is to recognize where he is working, and then follow the divine nudge to help others see it too.

NUDGE EVANGELISM

George Herbert, Anglican priest and poet, was close friends with Izaak Walton, the patron saint of fishing.[1] In his classic text, *The Country Parson*, Herbert described an effective minister as "a diligent observer and tracker of God's ways."[2]

Reflecting on this, Leonard Sweet said, "I am convinced that Herbert's phrase, 'a tracker of God's ways' is the essence of nudge evangelism."[3] This echoes a helpful motto gleaned from Henry Blackaby: Find out where God is at work and join him there.[4]

GOD WORKS THAT WAY

Before we can "track God's ways," there's an important issue to settle. Does our worldview leave room for the supernatural? Is God truly present and active in our lives? Can he really guide us by the Holy Spirit?

If you only listen to your rational side, the answer is no, and you won't see much in the supernatural department. You'll accomplish good things, of course, but won't experience anything marvelous. Those who believe in miracles are much more likely to experience them.

New Testament scholar Dr. Ken Schenck aptly noted, "There should be manifestations of God's power in signs and miracles all around us, if this thing we call Christianity is true."[5] Evangelism, by its very nature, is supernatural business. The apostle Paul expressed this in 1 Thessalonians 1:5: "Our gospel came to you not simply with words but also with power, with the Holy Spirit and deep conviction."

If you muster up enough faith to believe the supernatural is possible, you will be amazed to discover God really can work that way.

30
FISHING
WITH
JESUS

WHEN WE GO FISHING WITH JESUS FOR FISH, WE CATCH
LIVE ONES AND THEY DIE. WHEN WE GO FISHING WITH
JESUS
FOR MEN, WE CATCH DEAD ONES AND THEY LIVE.

Acts is a "fishing with Jesus" guidebook. We learn valuable lessons from these earliest anglers who "tracked God's ways" and experienced wonders. We can follow in their footsteps. Amazing things happen when we are ready, open, and willing for what God wants to do through us.

BE READY AND GOD WILL SEND THEM TO YOU

God will send lost treasures your way when you are ready for them. The first step in going fishing with Jesus is to prepare your own heart. This happened to Peter in Acts 10. He needed to deal with his own prejudice and legalism before God sent Cornelius to him. When Peter was ready, Cornelius arrived.

Get ready for the people God wants to send to you.

I'M READY PRAYER

Lord, I will receive each person I encounter
today as a gift from you. May I see them as
genuine treasures, and show them your love.
May each interaction be filled with grace.
Amen.

God sometimes sends unusual gifts. One Thursday morning, I said the "I'm Ready" prayer, and waited eagerly to see what treasures God had in store for me.

A very pregnant young lady stepped into my office, desperately searching for a pastor to perform an emergency wedding on Saturday. I could tell life had been hard for her, and this season was extremely stressful. To top it off, her fiancée was having tailbone surgery at that very moment.

"We can't afford anything, but really need to be married before the baby comes."

My extensive premarital counseling process normally would prohibit such a suggestion, but this time, the Holy Spirit nudged my heart and said, "These are my treasures. I am working in their lives. Bless them, and make them an exception to your rule."

She was overjoyed when I agreed to perform her wedding and amazed when I told her about my prayer that morning. She could hardly imagine herself as God's treasure.

On Saturday, the bride arrived at Hayward Beach, wearing a bright yellow maternity dress. "I didn't own a dress, so a friend loaned me hers," she beamed. "It's perfect. Yellow is my favorite color."

When the bride, in her yellow dress, wobbled with her hobbling groom to the shore of Lake Hayward, she burst into joyful tears. "Look what God did! He decorated my wedding with flowers!"

Sure enough, several bright yellow water lilies adorned the lake's edge, as if strategically arranged by heaven's wedding coordinator.

At that moment, I felt the Father's heart for his precious, wandering daughter, who now rejoiced in his goodness.

When we're ready, God sends all sorts of surprises.

BE OPEN AND GOD WILL GUIDE YOU TO THEM

As we're open to God's leading, he directs us to those who need his blessing most. This is what Philip did in Acts 8. Following a divine nudge, he traveled south down a desert road and discovered a spiritual seeker from Ethiopia. Because Philip was open, the Ethiopian eunuch experienced salvation and introduced the gospel to his native land.

I'M OPEN PRAYER

God, please guide me to someone who
needs to be reminded of your love. Help me
to be a blessing and encouragement.
Amen.

Praying, on my way to officiate the funeral of a suicide victim, I felt God wanted me to speak a blessing to a woman with platinum blonde hair.

The funeral home was crowded when I arrived, but I spotted her instantly and followed the nudge.

"Excuse me, this probably seems strange, but on my way here, I sensed I was supposed to bless and encourage someone with platinum blonde hair. You are the one who fits that description. So, can I give you a blessing?"

She stared at me like I was from Mars or had three heads.

I felt really stupid, but smiled and said, "May God bless you, keep you, and help you in every situation. May his comforting grace surround you like a blanket and warm your soul."

She seemed unnerved by the encounter and relieved when I left.

"Struck out there," I thought.

A few months later, I was at a convenience store, and the clerk said, "There you are. I've been looking for you!"

I didn't recognize her until she said, "Remember this?" and removed her hat.

It was the lady with platinum blonde hair.

"Of course, I remember."

"I thought what you said was so strange, but now I understand. Two weeks later my son committed suicide. I believe the Lord sent you ahead of time to give me strength for what I was about to face in my life."

BE WILLING AND GOD WILL USE YOU
TO MAKE A DIFFERENCE

Going fishing with Jesus requires risk. "For whoever wants to save their life will lose it," he said, "but whoever loses their life for me will find it" (Matt. 16:25). This is what Ananias did in Acts 9. He was at home, minding his own business, when God called him to go visit Saul, the persecutor of Christians. After a mild protest, Ananias went willingly and, as a result, changed the entire course of human history.

I'M WILLING PRAYER

Jesus, you gave your all for me. I give my
all for you. Whatever you ask, I will do today.
Wherever you direct, I will go. May I obey
your call, and consider no risk or
sacrifice too great.
Amen.

A few years ago, our community was traumatized when a ninety-three-year-old woman was stabbed fifteen times in a "thrill kill" slaying with satanic overtones. A young man, who described himself as "Satan's son," was arrested.

Upon hearing this horrific news, Pat, a gentle grandmother, felt a strong impression to visit the suspect, Christopher, in jail. When everyone else recoiled in horror, Pat took a risk and stepped courageously into his life. Compassion led the way, and she saw him as a human being, rather than the cold-blooded murderer portrayed in the media.

Pat visited Christopher regularly. She listened, shared Scriptures, and prayed with him. Eventually, through Pat's faithful influence, he surrendered his heart to Christ and was baptized.

No sin is too great to be forgiven. No one is too far from redemption. Regardless of how deep the sin, God's grace goes deeper still.

Because a grandmother was willing to *do* something, a "son of Satan" *became* something—a child of God.

31
A FRESH APPROACH
TO
EVANGELISM

MOST OF THE WORLD IS COVERED BY WATER.
A FISHERMAN'S JOB IS SIMPLE: PICK OUT THE BEST PARTS.

—CHARLES WATERMAN

For several years, I've taught evangelism for nontraditional ministerial students through the Wesleyan FLAME program. During every class, we spend one afternoon out in the community "doing the stuff." After studying the foundations, swapping stories, and receiving practical instruction, we're ready to go fishing with Jesus.

The approach I use in these classes is something I picked up from my sons who brought it home from trips to Mexico with

Adventures in Missions. They call it "ask the Lord time." I modified it, and gave it another name: treasure hunt (though I later discovered I wasn't the first person to have that idea).[1]

TREASURE HUNTS

Here's how the treasure hunt works: We spend about an hour alone in prayer, asking God to guide us to those who need blessing and encouragement and give us directions or clues so we can find them. Then we wait, listen, and jot down what comes to our minds.

Often, the prompting is toward a certain kind of place, such as a nursing home, hospital, or city park. Sometimes, it's a specific kind of person, like a single mother, elderly man, or teenager. Sometimes people receive a Scripture verse to share. Occasionally, the clues seem random and odd. We then group people together according to what we sense God is telling us and head out for an afternoon of treasure hunting.

GUIDELINES REGARDING IMPRESSIONS

A caution is in order. Without godly wisdom and solid biblical moorings, following impressions can disintegrate into nonsense. The following guidelines are helpful for seeking divine guidance and interpreting inner nudges.

Not Every Impression Is Guidance from God

John Wesley warned, "Do not hastily ascribe things to God."[2] Be careful in declaring "thus says the Lord." If it doesn't come true, you're a false prophet.

Test Your Impressions

Martin Wells Knapp proposed the following questions to help people discern whether or not their impulses are from above.[3]

- Is it scriptural? Is the impression in harmony with the Bible? God doesn't guide against his Word.
- Is it right? "Impressions which are from God are always right," Knapp said. "They may be contrary to our feelings, our prejudices and our natural inclinations, but they are always right. They will stand all tests."
- Is it providential? God opens a way for what he wants. You don't have to rush or push. His doors have automatic openers.
- Is it reasonable? Jesus died to take away our sins not our brains. He expects us to use the intelligence he gave us.

Play It Out Before You Toss It Out

This entire concept may seem odd to you. But before judging a nudge, play it out. Is this loving? Is it good? Does this grow your heart for others? Is it an act of faith? Will you bless somebody?

What harm will happen if you're wrong? If it's basically a blessing all the way around, go for it.

Remember What It's About

Treasure hunting is not about chasing clues. Rather, it is about finding the lost, broken, hurting people Christ treasures. The clues, somewhat like a high-stakes scavenger hunt, make the excursions fun, providing courage and great conversation starters for the teams as they go.

Every time, my students find treasure—and that's the point. They don't normally get every clue, but they always find someone who needs blessing and encouragement. The students always return rejoicing over what God did through them. Occasionally, the stories are mind-boggling.

A Few True Fish Tales

The accounts I share in the following chapter may be a bit wild for you. Don't fret. I'm not saying you need to do this. It's fine to stick with more conservative methods of sharing Jesus. After all, God's great work is normally done quietly without fireworks. However, I hope these evangelism adventures, like great fish stories from legendary anglers, capture your imagination and inspire hopeful possibilities.

32
PURPLE FISH
FISHING ADVENTURES

WHO SAYS FISHIN' AIN'T COOL?

—PETE MAINA

The following accounts are just a small sampling of the astounding things God did when my FLAME evangelism students went into the community for an afternoon of blessing and encouragement.

PEACHES AND SHEARS

The class laughed when Nick shared two strange words that came during his "ask the Lord time": *peaches* and *shears*.

Later that afternoon, Nick's group of treasure hunters ended up in a shopping mall. A classmate nudged Nick and said, "Hey, there's your shears!" A hair salon logo featured a big pair of scissors. "Why don't you go inside and see if you find peaches?"

So, Nick stepped into the salon and said, "Excuse me, I'm looking for peaches."

"Yep," responded one of the beauticians. "She's over there."

Nick's jaw dropped, "Really?"

He approached Peaches, and explained to the bewildered beautician the unusual prompting that led him to her. "Is there anything I can pray for you about?"

Peaches burst into tears and wrapped her arms around the surprised ministerial student.

A coworker smiled and said, "See, I told you God was real!"

Nick ran to get his classmates, who then gathered around Peaches and prayed with her. She was facing a difficult decision and running from God, but the hound of heaven used our crew to track her down.

HAMMERED METAL BUTTERFLY

In Michigan during his time of prayer, Bill pictured a butterfly made of hammered metal. He and a partner ended up searching for clues in Frankenmuth but found nothing. Discouraged, as the afternoon drew to an end, Bill gave up and decided to buy some candy.

The candy shop clerk, who handed him change, wore a butterfly ring made of hammered metal. Bill was so startled that he didn't know what to say and just walked out with his treats.

Immediately, he felt the Spirit's nudge (kick in the pants is more like it) to go back and talk with her. After whispering a quick prayer for help, Bill marched into shop and explained his mission.

"So, my treasure hunt led me to you this afternoon," he said. "Is there anything I can pray for you about?"

"Oh, my God!" the young lady exclaimed. "I am so lost!"

"Well, now you've been found!" Bill beamed.

Moments later, he prayed with the clerk, and she opened her life to Jesus. To top everything off, Bill knew a pastor from the same community where she lived and connected them.

IN THE SHADOW OF THE STEEPLE

Once, as we shared our clue lists, a guy blurted, "Krispy Kreme donuts!"

"Yeah, right," another student ribbed. "That's your tummy talking."

A couple of other clues were a troubled waitress and the shadow of a steeple.

Driving down the road, we spotted a Krispy Kreme, swung into the parking lot, and entered. A waitress stood behind the cash register. The steeple from the cathedral across the street cast a shadow directly over her. When we shared the clues that led us to her, the first thing this troubled waitress said was, "I definitely need prayer. My life is such a mess." As we gathered around to bless and encourage this dear soul, she wept, realizing how deeply God treasured her.

SINGLE McDONALD'S MOM

In Denton, Maryland, a group of treasure hunters searched for a single mom, a grocery store, McDonald's, and "someone wrestling with God." Also, Peggi had a generous gift to deliver. She recently inherited some money and felt God wanted her to use five hundred dollars to bless somebody in need. (Several students in the class suggested that they might be that somebody, but Peggi was too savvy for that.)

The group ended up at Food Lion, looking for a single mom who needed five hundred dollars. They found her in the checkout line, dressed in a McDonald's uniform. Stepping up behind her, Peggi said, "Excuse me, can we buy your groceries?"

The startled woman couldn't understand why on earth anyone would pay her grocery bill, which totaled one hundred fifty dollars.

After the group lugged groceries to her car, the young woman explained that she is a single mom with four kids and a very tight budget. This was her first day of work at McDonald's.

In the parking lot, the conversation went deep, as she shared her struggles: "I quit going to church because I've been angry and wrestling with God."

"The Lord sent us here to remind you of how deeply he loves you," Peggi said. "He will help you through this situation and every other problem you face."

The team surrounded their new friend and prayed with her to stop wrestling and start resting in Jesus. She nearly passed out when they handed her the extra three hundred fifty dollars for good measure.

CRUISING WITH JESUS IN A PINK CADILLAC

Roland, a Haitian pastor from Philadelphia, and I ended up as treasure hunt partners in Frankfort, Indiana. Neither of us had a vehicle. "Use mine," a classmate offered, tossing us keys to her pink Cadillac.

Roland and I went cruising in the pink Caddy, looking for laundry and a Hispanic young man in blue jeans. We saw a guy who fit the description, carrying a clothes basket into Frankfort Cleaners. I swung into the lot, and Roland jumped from the car before it stopped. He ran to the guy and started speaking in Spanish. I had no idea Roland knew Spanish!

WE'RE NOT GOING TO CATCH FISH if WE DON'T fishing"

The young man didn't appreciate the intrusion. He shook his fists, cursed loudly at Roland, and told him to mind his own business.

"Wrong guy," Roland said when he climbed back into the pink Cadillac.

"Now what do we do?" I wondered.

"We wait here for the right guy," said Roland.

So we waited, and in about ten minutes, another Hispanic young man in blue jeans showed up with a basket.

"That's our guy!" Roland said, and he went after him.

They talked for a long time while I watched from the car. I saw the young man wipe tears, as they bowed their heads in prayer.

This was his second day in the US. The poor guy was lost, homesick, and afraid. Roland encouraged him and directed him to Templo de Poder, a congregation only a few blocks away, where he could find loving support and fellowship.

THE DARKEST PLACE

I spent an afternoon in a tavern with a group of ministerial students after following clues to "the darkest place in town." This experience was a huge stretch for some of them (similar to the stretch unchurched people feel when visiting church for the first time). We ordered soft drinks and, after obtaining permission, talked with people about Jesus.

Over the next couple of hours, we engaged in several significant (and a few incoherent) conversations and prayed with a dozen people. As we prepared to leave, the bartender said, "What you folks are doing is good. I wish there was more of that in this world." Then he picked up our tab after we prayed with him.

POCONOS PARK BENCH

A group of students followed clues to a bench on a hiking trail in the Poconos. They approached a couple and shared their mission of blessing and encouragement.

"Leave us alone! You stupid religious kooks really annoy me!" the guy growled. "I don't even believe in God!"

His shocked girlfriend said, "But . . . Larry, that's not what you told me this morning."

Over an hour later, our group passed the same couple who were still in heated discussion, sitting on a park bench.

Did God send our little posse along to reveal what was really in Larry's heart?

CHRIST AT THE CROSSROADS

Chuck and I ended up together on a treasure hunt in South Carolina looking for "someone at the crossroads." We found a fellow who had just been fired and encouraged him. We picked up a man walking to the pharmacy to buy medicine for his dying father. We helped a guy get to the courthouse in time to avoid a bench warrant arrest. We happened upon the scene of an auto accident, provided assistance, directed traffic, comforted the rattled victims, and even swept broken glass from the street. Driving back to the campus, Chuck and I both agreed, "Now, that was fantastic fishing!

6/23/24

Purposeful... Are doing this on purpose? Are we looking for and asking God for opportunities?

Planting seeds...

The plan of salvation...

Evangelism is a process, not an event, at least for most.

33
GO FISH

BUT WE, WHO HAVE UNDERTAKEN GOD, CAN NEVER FIN-
ISH.

—RAINER MARIA RILKE

You go nowhere by accident," said former US Senate Chaplain Richard Halverson. "Wherever you go, God is sending you."[1] Keep this in mind. With the right focus, life is one big mission trip. Be prepared for divine appointments all along the way.

Here are a dozen final purple fish fishing tips for sharing God's grace.

FIVE-DAY BLESSING PROJECT

For five days, first thing in the morning, pray this prayer: "Lord, please send me to someone you treasure today so I can be a source of encouragement and blessing. Help me receive all those you send into my life today as a gift." Then, keep your eyes wide open. After five days, you might want to keep going.

KINGDOM EYES

Spend time on intentional prayer walks and/or drives. As you move slowly through the neighborhood, ask God to show you the community through kingdom eyes. May you see your neighbors the way Jesus sees them.

GOD POCKET

This is a delightful idea proposed by Bruce Wilkinson. Prayerfully set apart a specific amount of money for your "God pocket." The money belongs to the Lord and is to be used as he directs. You will receive a nudge from the Holy Spirit when it's time to pass it along.[2]

SOCIAL MEDIA

Use your social media accounts to put in a good plug for Jesus, without being pushy or preachy. Sites such as Facebook and Twitter provide a wonderful platform for sharing Christ's love in winsome ways.

TREASURE HUNT

Take a few brave friends on a treasure hunt, similar to what was described in the last chapter. If you prayerfully seek God's guidance, he will lead you to those who need his grace. Who knows what kind of adventures you may experience?

HOSPITALITY

Open up your life and home to someone who does not share your spiritual beliefs. Your kitchen, ping pong table, canoe, or basketball hoop can be a tremendous evangelism tool.

ACTS OF SERVICE

Invite nonbelievers to go with you on missions of mercy. It will give them a taste of serving God by blessing others. Ruth Tucker calls this "friendship evangelism in reverse."[3]

NONTHREATENING ENVIRONMENTS

Create environments where nonbelievers can come without feeling threatened or judged. For instance, guys who show no interest in church may eagerly accept an invitation to go fishing. Josh Hunt nails it when he writes, "People who are opposed to the gospel are not opposed to ice cream."[4]

LITTLE MISSION TRIPS

When you enter a store, think of it as a mission trip. Go intentionally, seeking someone to bless and encourage. I've had numerous God-encounters and prayer meetings over the years in shopping aisles when I went into the store on a mission.

GIFTING

Generosity blesses people. Tangible expressions of care speak deeply. Carole bakes cookies for her neighbors. Jim gives senior citizens rides to medical appointments. Frank teaches kids to fish. Stacy collects picture books for underprivileged children. Jon mentors a troubled boy. Linda provides refreshments for teenagers. Bonnie knits prayer shawls. Ed and Todd take inner-city teens on wilderness canoe adventures. What do you have in your hand? Use it to bless others.

PRAYER TRIAD

Enlist two friends to join you in a prayer covenant. Each person lists three friends who need Jesus, and all three of you pray for these nine friends every day. Then, look for opportunities to share Christ's love with them. Your mutual prayers will pave the way.

TWO BIG QUESTIONS

Each evening, ask yourself two big questions: How did I show God's love today? And what can I do tomorrow?

BYZANTINE BENEDICTION

"Go now with God. Be not tempted to stay in the safety of known places. Move from where you are to where God points. . . . Be not tempted to go only in your time, when it suits, when it is sure. . . . Choose not to go alone. Go in the faith that there is no wilderness so vast, no way so confused, that God is not already there to show you the way."[5]

In other words . . . go fish!

NOTES

Chapter 1

1. Rebecca Manley Pippert, *Out of the Saltshaker & Into the World: Evangelism as a Way of Life*, 2nd ed. (Downers Grove, IL: InterVarsity, 1999), 15.

Chapter 2

1. Norman Maclean, *A River Runs through It* (Chicago: University of Chicago Press, 1989), 1.

2. Gail Godwin, *Evensong* (New York: Ballantine, 1999), 27–28.

Chapter 3

1. I picked this up years ago from my friend Tom Raven, who heard it twenty-five years ago at a youth club in Moreno Valley, California. Attempts to find the original source have been unsuccessful.

2. Andrews and Abrahams were a part of the G.R.A.D.E. Program, an effective evangelism training resource invented by John Maxwell. In its season, many came to Christ as a result of G.R.A.D.E., and the failure mentioned here was mostly in the way I applied it.

Chapter 4

1. Thomas Neely Ralston, a Methodist theologian, wrote *Elements of Divinity* in 1924. The four points are my own interpretation of what he shared.

2. Elena Mannes, *Amazing Grace with Bill Moyers: The Story of a Song That Makes a Difference*, PBS, 1990.

3. John Newton, "Amazing Grace," 1779, public domain, accessed February 11, 2014, http://www.hymntime.com/tch/htm/a/m/a/amazing_grace.htm.

4. This phrase, from a John W. Peterson hymn later borrowed by David Crowder, was based on the testimony of Old Jim at the Montrose Bible Conference in 1961, accessed February 11, 2014, http://wordwise hymns.com/2010/11/01/today-in-1921-john-peterson-born.

Chapter 5

1. Early church father, Tertullian (A.D. 155–245), in his short treatise "On Baptism," accessed January 16, 2014, http://www.tertullian.org/articles/souter_orat_bapt/souter_orat_bapt_04baptism.htm.

2. I swiped this phrase from Brian McLaren's theology and fly fishing group: Brian D. McLaren, "Yellowstone" (blog), http://brianmclaren.net/archives/blog/yellowstone.html.

3. *Legendary* has two meanings, and I mean both. Controversy surrounds Hayward's world-record muskies caught by Louis Spray and Cal Johnson. Detractors have a compelling case, but that's not my fight. Bogus or not, their pikes were much bigger than anything I've ever landed.

4. Larry Ramsell is the author of the authoritative two-volume set *A Compendium of Muskie Angling History* (Hayward, WI: House of Muskies Publications, 2007). He wrote of the "muskie mystique" in volume two. Note that he correctly spells it with an "-ie" rather than a "-y." He explained that *musky* equals smell and *muskie* equals fish. However, in this book, I chose the spelling that smells because it is more common.

5. Joseph Scriven, "What a Friend We Have in Jesus," 1855, public domain, accessed February 11, 2014, http://www.cyber hymnal.org/htm/w/ a/f/wafwhij.htm.

Chapter 6

1. Isaac Watts, "When I Survey the Wondrous Cross," 1707, public domain, accessed February 11, 2014, http://www.cyber hymnal.org/htm/w/ h/e/whenisur.htm.

2. I gleaned the upward, inward, and outward journey idea from Henri Nouwen, *Reaching Out: The Three Movements of the Spiritual Life* (Garden City, NY: Image, 1986).

3. Mark Batterson's Facebook page, accessed April 28, 2013, https://www.facebook.com/markbatterson/posts/101516644019 58140.

4. "The Gaze of the Soul" is the title of a chapter in A. W. Tozer's *The Pursuit of God*.

5. Richard Baxter, *The Reformed Pastor*, public domain, accessed January 16, 2014, http://www.ccel.org/ccel/baxter/ pastor.txt.

Chapter 8

1. Festo Kivengere, "Incarnation," quoted by Steve Aronowitz (blog), December 25, 2009, http://stevearonowitz.wordpress.com/2009/12/25/incarnation-god-is-love-rushing-on-a-rescue-mission.

2. Rumi, Good Reads, accessed January 16, 2014, http://www.goodreads.com/quotes/8521-where-there-is-ruin-there-is-hope-for-a-treasure.

Chapter 9

1. Gerard Manley Hopkins, "As Kingfishers Catch Fire," Poetry Foundation, accessed January 16, 2014, http://www.poetry foundation.org/poem/173654.

2. Eli Stanley Jones, *Conversion* (Nashville, TN: Abingdon, 1959), 221.

Chapter 10

1. Bill Hybels and Mark Mittleberg, *Becoming a Contagious Christian* (Grand Rapids, MI: Zondervan, 1994), 18–24.

2. Rick Warren's Twitter feed, accessed November 7, 2013, https://twitter.com/RickWarren/status/398546868428603392.

Chapter 11

1. Kevin Dedmon, *The Ultimate Treasure Hunt: A Guide to Supernatural Evangelism through Supernatural Encounters* (Shippensburg, PA: Destiny Image, 2007), 17.

Chapter 12

1. Philip Yancey, *Grace Notes: Daily Readings with a Fellow Pilgrim* (Grand Rapids, MI: Zondervan, 2009), 177.

2. John H. Stockton, "Come Every Soul by Sin Oppressed," *Salvation Melodies No. 1* (Philadelphia: Perkinpine & Higgins, 1874), http://www.hymntime.com/tch/htm/c/o/m/comesbso.htm.

Chapter 13

1. This concept comes from Robert T. Rush, "From Pearl Merchant to Treasure Hunter: The Missionary Yesterday and Today," *Catholic Mind* 76 (1978): 6–10.

2. B. T. Roberts, "A Fighting Holiness—Sanctification in Streams," *Holiness Teachings: The Life and Work of B. T. Roberts* (North Chili, NY: Earnest Christian, 1893), accessed January 17, 2014, http://www.ccel.org/ccel/roberts_bh/holiness.xxx.html.

Chapter 14

1. Wesley Duewel, *Touch the World through Prayer* (Grand Rapids, MI: Zondervan, 1986), 23.

2. Ed Silvoso, *Prayer Evangelism: How to Change the Spiritual Climate over Your Home, Neighborhood and City* (Ventura, CA: Regal, 2000), 35.

Chapter 15

1. Missiologist James Engel invented a scale that demonstrates the process of spiritual readiness. It was first introduced in James Engel and Wilbert Norton, *What's Gone Wrong with the Harvest? A Communication Strategy for the Church and World Evangelism* (Grand Rapids, MI: Zondervan, 1975).

2. William Fay, *Share Jesus without Fear* (Nashville: B&H, 1999), 11.

3. Francis Thompson, "The Hound of Heaven," *The Oxford Book of English Mystical Verse*, eds. D. Nicholson and A. Lee (Oxford: Clarendon, 1917).

4. I found this fisherman's prayer posted in a friend's cabin. Original source unknown.

Chapter 16

1. Marshall Shelley, *Well-Intentioned Dragons: Ministering to Problem People in the Church* (Minneapolis: Bethany, 1994).

2. Watchman Nee, *Sit, Walk, Stand* (Carol Stream, IL: Tyndale, 1977), 20.

3. Adelle Banks, "Study: Youth See Christians as Judgmental, Anti-Gay," *USA Today*, October 10, 2007, http://usatoday30.usa today.com/news/religion/2007-10-10-christians-young_N.htm.

4. Ann Voskamp, "How the Hidden Dangers of Comparison are Killing Us . . . {and Our Daughters}: The Measuring Stick Principle," *A Holy Experience* (blog), November 6, 2013, http://www.aholyexperience.com/2013/11/how-the-hidden-dangers-of-comparison-are-killing-us-and-our-daughters-the-measuring-stick-principle.

5. Leonard Sweet, *Nudge: Awakening Each Other to the God Who's Already There* (Colorado Springs: David C. Cook, 2010), 69.

Chapter 17

1. Keith Drury, e-mail message to author, September 29, 2013. Keith borrowed this concept from Dennis F. Kinlaw.

2. Meister Eckhart, *Sermons & Treatises, Volume 1*, trans. and ed. M. O'C. Walshe, excerpt, accessed January 17, 2014, http://www.beshara.org/principles/selected-reading/meister-eckhart-2.html.

Chapter 18

1. David Gibbons, *The Monkey and the Fish: Liquid Leadership for a Third-Culture Church* (Grand Rapids, MI: Zondervan, 2009), 17.

Chapter 19

1. Jonathan Buckland, e-mail messge to author, October 28, 2013.

2. Mary Schaller and the folks at Q Place (www.qplace.com) call these nine practices "The Arts of Spiritual Conversations." With these practices and tools to start ongoing discussions about God, Q Place empowers Christians to engage in meaningful conversations about God and the Bible with people who believe differently. Instead of promoting gospel presentations, Q Place equips Christians to build relationships and have spiritual conversations

with those outside the church. It's surprisingly simple, and it's what Jesus did.

3. Peter Scazerro, *Emotionally Healthy Spirituality: Unleash the Power of Authentic Life in Christ* (Nashville: Thomas Nelson, 2006), 183.

Chapter 20

1. C. S. Lewis, *The Problem of Pain* (New York: HarperOne, 2001), 91.

2. A wonderful account of Hitchens's conversion can be found at "How I Found God and Peace with My Atheist Brother: Peter Hitchens Traces His Journey Back to Christianity," *Daily Mail*, December 16, 2001, http://www.dailymail.co.uk/news/article-1255983/How-I-God-peace-atheist-brother-PETER-HITCHENS-traces-journey-Christianity.html.

3. Sigurd Olson, "We Need Wilderness," *National Parks Magazine*, January–March 1946, accessed January 17, 2014, http://www4.uwm.edu/letsci/research/sigurd_olson/articles/1940s/1946-01-00 — We%20Need%20WildernessNational%20Parks%20Mag.htm.

4. C. S. Lewis, *Screwtape Letters* (New York: HarperCollins, 1996), 156.

Chapter 21

1. Gary Chapman, *Now You're Speaking My Language: Honest Communication and Deeper Intimacy for a Stronger Marriage* (Nashville: B&H, 2007), 25–35.

2. R. A. Torrey, quoted in Alvin Reid's, *Introduction to Evangelism* (Nashville: B&H, 1998), 221.

3. Miroslav Volf's Facebook page, January 16, 2012, https://www.facebook.com/permalink.php?story_fbid=2993478 76779169&id=100001118779221.

Chapter 22

1. Christian Piatt, "The Dangers of Evangelism," *Huffington Post*, November 27, 2012, http://www.huffingtonpost.com/christian-piatt/the-dangers-of-evangelism_b_2192677.html.

2. Airdre Grant, "Spirituality, Health, and the Complementary Medicine Practitioner," *Journal of the Australian Traditional Medicine Society*, December 1, 2007, http://www.thefreelibrary.com/Spirituality,+health+and+the+complementary+medicine+practitioner.-a0173677448.

3. John Ortberg, "Category Confusion," *Leadership Journal*, June 14, 2010, http://www.christianitytoday.com/le/2010/june-online-only/categoryconfusion.html?start=2.

Chapter 23

1. This quote has been attributed to various sources.

Chapter 24

1. There is no historical evidence that St. Francis actually said "Preach the gospel at all times, and when necessary, use words." However, the quote is commonly attributed to him, and

people frequently use him to justify why they never speak up for Jesus. In reality, St. Francis preached with both life and words. See http://thegospelcoalition.org/blogs/tgc/2012/07/11/fact checkermisquoting-francis-of-assisi/.

2. Scot McKnight, "Is It Still Evangelism if There Are No Words?" *Outreach Magazine*, August 21, 2013, http://www.out reachmagazine.com/features/5052-is-it-still-evangelism-if-there-are-no-words.html.

3. "Penn Jillette Gets a Gift of a Bible," YouTube video, posted August 4, 2009, http://www.youtube.com/watch?v= ZhG-tkQ_Q2w.

Chapter 25

1. Ram Dass and Paul Gorman, *How Can I Help? Stories and Reflections on Service* (New York: Knopf, 1985), 62.

Chapter 26

1. Dorothy Bernard, Good Reads, accessed January 17, 2014, http://www.goodreads.com/quotes/55811-courage-is-fear-that-has-said-its-prayers.

2. Oblates of St. Francis de Sales, accessed January 17, 2014, http://www.oblates.org/ dss/francis.

3. Craig Groeschel, "They Aren't All Saved," *Swerve*, April 2, 2009, http://swerve.lifechurch.tv/2009/04/02/they-all-aren't-saved.

4. There are many variations of this phrase. Attempts to find the original source have been unsuccessful.

5. Martin Luther King, Jr., "Antidotes to Fear," The King Center, September 13, 2012, http://www.thekingcenter.org/blog/mlk-quote-week-building-dikes-courage.

Chapter 27

1. Leonard Sweet, *Nudge: Awakening Each Other to the God Who's Already There* (Colorado Springs: David C. Cook, 2010), 127.

2. I gleaned this concept from my psychologist friend, Damian Vraniak, *Maps & Metaphors of the Human Heart: 1, 2, 3, Mystery, Me, Myself and I* (Hayward, WI: Whitewolf Press, 2009), 223–227.

Chapter 28

1. My inclusion of Louis Spray's fishing advice is for practical purposes only, and not an endorsement of him or his claims. Much controversy surrounds his fish weighing sixty-nine pounds and eleven ounces. That's not my fight. I'll let people smarter than me sort it out.

2. John Dettloff, *Topwater Tactics & Tales: A Guide to Using Surface Baits for Musky* (Couderay, WI: Trail's End, 2004), 238.

3. Ibid.

4. Ibid.

5. Leonard Sweet, *Nudge: Awakening Each Other to the God Who's Already There* (Colorado Springs: David C. Cook, 2010), 28–29.

6. Dettloff, *Topwater*, 122.

7. T. S. Eliot, "East Coker," in *Four Quartets* (Orlando: Harcourt, 1971), 31.

8. Michael Cooper-White, "On Fishing and Spirituality," *Lutheran Theological Seminary at Gettysburg*, February 16, 2011, http://www.ltsg.edu/Publications/From-the-Gettysburg-PO/February-2011/On-Fishing-and-Spirituality.

Chapter 29

1. The warm relationship between Izaak Walton and George Herbert is described in Stapleton Martin, *Izaak Walton and His Friends*, 2nd ed. (London: Chapman & Hall, 1904).

2. George Herbert, *Country Parson: His Character and Rule of Holy Life* (Boston: James B. Dow, 1841), 31.

3. Leonard Sweet, *Nudge: Awakening Each Other to the God Who's Already There* (Colorado Springs: David C. Cook, 2010), 278.

4. This is the theme of Blackaby's book, *Experiencing God: Knowing and Doing the Will of God* (Nashville: B&H, 1990).

5. Ken Schenck, "Sermon Starters: 21st Century Evangelism," *Common Denominator* (blog), April 25, 2009, http://ken schenck.blogspot.com/ 2009/04/sermon-starters-21st-century-evangelism.html.

Chapter 31

1. Kevin Dedmon, a pastor of Bethel Church in Redding, California, wrote *The Ultimate Treasure Hunt: A Guide to Supernatural Evangelism through Supernatural Encounters* (Shippensburg, PA: Destiny Image, 2007). His approach is much more along a prophetic or word of knowledge line than mine.

2. John Wesley, *A Plain Account of Christian Perfection* (New York: G. Lane & P. P. Sanford, 1844), 42.

3. Martin Wells Knapp, *Impressions*, Wesleyan Heritage Library (Cincinnati: Revivalist Publishing House, 1892), accessed January 17, 2014, http://media.sabda.org/alkitab-6/wh2-hdm/hdm0115.pdf.

Chapter 33

1. Richard Halverson, "You Go Nowhere by Accident," *The Story* (blog), September 30, 3013, http://apcthestory.word press.com/tag/richard-halverson.

2. Bruce Wilkinson writes about this concept in *You Were Made for This: Seven Keys to a Life of Predictable Miracles* (Colorado Springs: Multnomah, 2009); and *The God Pocket: He Owns It. You Carry It. Suddenly Everything Changes* (Colorado Springs: Multnomah, 2011).

3. Ruth Tucker, *Left Behind Churches in a Megachurch World: How God Works through Ordinary Churches* (Grand Rapids, MI: Baker, 2006), 199–200.

4. Josh Hunt, "Ice Cream and Evangelism," *Good Questions Have Groups Talking* (blog), October 9, 2012, http://www.josh hunt.com/2012/10/ice-cream-and-evangelism.

5. Right Reverend Russell E. Jacobus used this beautiful benediction in "Bishop's Pastoral Address—2013," accessed January 17, 2014, http://www.episcopalfonddulac.org/documents/publications/pastoral2013.pdf.

Serve in the Overflow
of God's Love

Thirsty people are looking to the church for fountains of life-giving water. Too often, they find leaky buckets instead. Pastor Mark O. Wilson says it's time for the church to rise up in the power of the Holy Spirit to serve this present age. In *Filled Up, Poured Out*, he challenges and inspires pastors—and all Christians—to prepare their hearts to be filled with the Holy Spirit, so that they can in turn pour out God's presence, promise, peace, and power in their congregations and communities.

Filled with personal, inspirational stories from Mark's experience with growing a thriving congregation in a Wisconsin Northwoods town, this book will inspire you to seek the replenishing waters of God's Spirit and show you the pathway to revival for your parched soul.

Filled Up, Poured Out
978-0-89827-527-8
978-0-89827-715-9 (e-book)

1.800.493.7539 wphstore.com